MAGICKAL DESTINY

EXPERIENCE THE POWER OF YOUR
HOLY GUARDIAN ANGEL

DAMON BRAND

THE GALLERY OF
MAGICK

Contents

Blissful Destiny

For most people, life is chaos. It's a string of weird struggles and problems with barely a moment to reach for the destiny you want. You may be tossed and flung through accidents, mistakes, and more suffering than you deserve.

With magick, you tame the chaos. You choose the direction of your life. There is no destiny laid out for you to follow. There is no sequence of fated events that you are doomed to struggle through. With magick, you get to say what happens, how it happens, and how your life works out. Destiny is your choice.

With this book, you get a way of working that can inspire, change, or expand the fundamental themes of your existence. This is not about patching up problems or attracting a little more of what you need. It's about crafting reality to meet your deepest needs.

There are hundreds of books on magick with thousands of spells and rituals. There's so much choice, it can be overwhelming, and you don't know where to begin. It's time to offer you something different, something deeper. By using a sequence of magickal Protocols, you can make contact with your Holy Guardian Angel. You will gain a direct awareness of the spirit that watches over you.

Your Guardian Angel is already with you, already listening to your heart and soul, knowing your thoughts, your desires, and your dreams. When you act in ways that align you with angelic contact, awareness of your Angel will increase. The magick you discover in this book will enhance the connection and make it complete.

This book isn't quite like anything else we've published. You might have come here hoping for the next super-fast ritual that gets results in ten minutes. We are aware of the huge push in the occult community to make magick incredibly easy and fast. We know about it because we have published many books that introduced those techniques. Part of the revolution has been to strip away ceremony and make pure, simple magick that works. But we also know that more promises of 'faster and better' are not the way forward.

I cannot offer you a quick method to cheat your way to the Angel with a few simple rituals and a set of pretty sigils. That's not what you need, and it's not how this process works. Although there are sigils in this book that can help to inspire your connection to the Angel, there is so much more to the magick. It's time to go deeper, so that there is more fundamental power built into your very existence. In time, using the secrets in this book, magickal effects can occur without you even having to perform any rituals. This makes it one of the most powerful ways to integrate magick into your life, so that desires manifest and results occur with nothing more than an act of choice.

Be in no doubt; this is a book of practical magick, and magick that works more effortlessly and fundamentally than anything else we have revealed before. I know the title is not as catchy as something like *Magickal Cashbook*, which makes you think about the thrills of instant money. The title of this book is ironic because you aren't seeking a destiny that was laid out for you by a higher power. You are choosing your destiny, based on what you discover to be the best way to live your life. Magick will guide you to find this destiny. Magick will empower you to make that destiny become real.

If you have ever read anything about the Holy Guardian Angel, you may be wondering if it can be possible to discover a method that makes contact real, in a safe and reliable way. It has long been said that a connection with the Holy Guardian Angel is only possible after months or years of extreme magick, with horrendous disruption and withdrawal from ordinary life, using a highly specific and tiresome ritual practice. Thankfully, that is not true.

I believe that the moment you reach out to the Angel, contact becomes real, and you can begin to obtain magickal benefits almost immediately. Disruption is not required.

The traditional practices were gruelling and often failed. What you discover in this book makes the process easier and more enjoyable. Your spiritual quest becomes a pleasant and beneficial journey of bliss rather than a foreboding challenge.

In some ways, this is the easiest magick you will ever find. It may appear slight, lacking in drama, and not quite what you expect, but this magick brings a conscious and deliberate connection to your Angel that makes all of life easier. Your connection to the magick will require your focus and commitment, but the rewards are always worthwhile.

The experience of Complete Contact, with visible appearance and direct communication with your Angel, requires dedication and time. I cannot change that, and there is no reason to do so. I can, however, help you increase the speed with which you encounter benefits from the initial stages of the magick.

This book is not an attempt to turn you into a mystical hermit. For me, the benefits of magick must apply in the real world. Everything I share with you here can enhance your life without you becoming an obsessed occultist.

The Angel is a source of protection and will guide you in a safe manner as soon as you begin to use the Protocols and methods I describe. The book is relatively short, by design, and will provide you with everything you need for this magickal work.

I try to keep a gentle sense of humour when I write, and although this is a serious subject, it doesn't need to be pompous or elitist. So often, when you read about the Angel, you feel certain that the author was definitely wearing white robes while writing on ancient parchment, with a quill, in a room full of incense. I want to be more down-to-earth. Part of what we're doing here is revealing this magick in a way that makes it workable. You are bringing your Angel down to earth.

For some people, seeking contact with the Holy Guardian Angel is a lifelong dream. For others, it's a curiosity, and a few have no interest, but I hope this book will show that even if you don't seek Complete Contact, the Angel can help you in many unexpected ways.

There are several ways to use this book. You can use it quite lightly, to obtain a general sense of your Angel and to see how this strengthens your ability to adapt reality to your needs. Or you can work more consistently, attempting to make the contact more tangible. Some readers will want to take this work to its limit, so that Complete Contact is achieved. You choose how to work with the Protocols and decide what you want to gain. I will guide you through this as we move through the book, and you will develop a strong intuition about what is right for you. You can work with the magick as intensely or casually as you please, allowing the power to surge or flow rapidly or gently.

I often say that the Angel can come to you without any magick at all. If you want to make contact, all you need is sincere desire and intention. You don't need any methods; you will find your way. That's every human's right, and everybody has the ability. Many Western occultists will say this is sacrilege, but all cultures and magickal traditions have their ways of obtaining a connection to the Angel. It is arrogant foolishness to assume that there could only be one form of 'high ceremonial magick' that could make this connection. Billions of people would be left out, and that isn't the case.

Your Angel is present and only needs you to become aware of its presence. That is the only secret you need. The everyday, the commonplace, the ordinary; that is where we are most of the time, and it is in the moments of our ordinary existence, our humble reality, that we can catch a glimpse of the Angel that is already with us. This glimpse can lead to a direct connection.

Some people will dismiss what I say as a soft, weak, New Age attempt at watering down the grand traditions of magick. There is no need for anybody to be defensive. I am not dismissing the other methods, and if you like them, that's fine, but I will offer another way, and if you want to begin the journey now, you can. But I should say that if you've come here looking for a new version of the traditional methods – often referred to as *The Abramelin* – you will be disappointed. If you're looking for a new way to do The Bornless Ritual, that's not what you get here. I am not rehashing that old work. If you like the old methods, please use them, but know that this book shares an entirely different set of Protocols designed to make contact safe and more rewarding.

I should stress the importance of safety because I know that some will call this book misguided or even dangerous in an attempt to make it appear sinister. This is normal with a magick book of any kind, but because this book has been so highly anticipated by a number of readers who follow my work, I want to be clear about the faith I have in this approach. I doubt this will be a popular book because the subject matter is esoteric, but I do not want enthusiastic seekers to be dismayed or discouraged when others dismiss its value. My ego can handle the negative wailing, but I hope you have the courage to trust your own instincts regarding the work. That is how magick should be. I don't own magick, and I am not a guru. But I have been working with magick for around forty years, and I believe that for you, this could be one of the most exciting adventures in practical magick.

Many occultists believe that contacting the Angel is the most important work of magick. Others, strangely enough, say it is something you should get out of the way early and move on from as soon as possible. Most people who have achieved Complete Contact agree that your life is never the same again, and your ability to know yourself and to work effective magick is strengthened when you have an awareness of your Angel.

Summarizing all the benefits you can gain from connecting with your Angel is beyond the ability of any writer, although you will gain more ideas about this as you read on. By moving through the book and being open to new ideas, you should begin to sense the level of power I am talking about. If you have never worked with magick at all, this book can be a good place to begin your exploration. If you are experienced, it can be a new way to survey the possibilities and expand your power.

I should also say that if you believe you have already made contact with your Angel using any other methods, this book can still be useful to you. This magick should help you to refine and strengthen your experience of the Angel.

I hope the book is as entertaining as it is useful, and please know that everything you read is included for a reason. I will not waste one moment of your time with superfluous anecdotes, but I will tell you stories of magick. There is great power in a story, and you can trust that when I talk about my experiences or recount the tales of other people, I am not filling pages for the sake of thickening the book. Every story reveals truth. Every word counts. Ideas may seem unclear at times, even contradictory, or repeated too often, but you can trust that everything has been set out this way with intention. When there is repetition, it is with great purpose. When you are made to pause and think, that is for a good reason. In reading, you undergo an opening to the experience of the Angel.

We have often told people to read our books thoroughly, and this may sound like a boring old lecture, with some stuffy teacher telling you to do your homework properly. The truth is probably more interesting. On a basic, practical level, there is no substitute for reading thoroughly and understanding fully. From the questions we receive, we know that the majority of problems and missteps are caused by readers rushing through the books and missing out some important bits. That's the mundane truth, but it goes further than that.

Our books were written by authors from The Gallery of Magick to convey what has been learned and tested over the last several decades, based on foundations of ancient knowledge and well-preserved secrets. And yet, they were not written merely as a way of communicating magickal techniques. We have used magick to create books that are, in themselves, part of a magickal process. When you read these books in full, you encounter patterns of words that help connect you to the magick. I share this to help open you to the power that lies within these words. I make this offering so that when you sense something happening as you read, you know it is more than your imagination.

You do not need belief or faith when you set out on this journey to the Angel. You only need an open mind and a little curiosity. Whatever you believe, if you are willing to try this magick, easily and gently, it can begin solving problems and easing your desires into place, almost without effort. I believe this can be one of the most exciting journeys in magick, but I want you to be the one who decides on its value, unflustered by my words or the opinions, doubts, and fears of others. Let your experience be the guide.

The Offer

In a wonderful post on the Gallery of Magick website, Adam Blackthorne asked what magick is for, and although it was something we had discussed at length over the years, I found his written response to that question to be a beautiful revelation. He pointed out that magick is sometimes approached out of curiosity, but usually for solving a problem, seeking more, and occasionally, to change your destiny. And he pointed out that no matter how hard you work, without magick, you can be disadvantaged. As he put it, 'Great artists remain undiscovered. Brilliant scientists fail to get a grant. The love of your life hurts you more than you believed possible. And plain old bad luck can kick you in the teeth over and over again. Life is random and chaotic unless you tame the chaos. If you believe in magick, you have a way. Something that goes beyond effort and struggle. It's a direct method of causing the change you crave.' I tried to echo those words in the opening to this book.

Adam went on to say that magick is not meant to solve every problem. It isn't for everything, but it can be used for anything. Although magick is still used by many to make ends meet, it can also be used to discover your purpose, and shift from solving problems to crafting and creating your life. This is what it is to control your destiny.

Furthermore, Adam went on to say that magick isn't always easy because some people start out from a place of catastrophe, poverty, or other circumstances that are incredibly difficult to modify, with or without magick. He said, 'Things work out if you persist, but even if you're doing well, you'll make mistakes because magick exists in the real world, not a fantasy world. This is all ok, and with magick at hand, you can recover more rapidly when things get messed up.'

And so, he concludes, we write about magick in all its forms for those who are drawn to magick. It is not for everybody, but if you find yourself attracted to the concept of magick, if you find yourself believing in magick, or if magick has always been part of your life, what we offer are new ways into magick that can be easier than anything that has gone before. That has never been truer than with the subject of the Guardian Angel.

We have aimed to share the simplifications we discovered. That has been our purpose. Not to create a revolution or usher in an age of ultra-simple magick, but to show that when crafted with great integrity, effective magick does not need to be dressed up in theory, ceremony, dogma, or worst of all, gurus and personalities.

Our purpose was never to share every single thing that we had discovered about magick. Our purpose was to show what we've simplified and made accessible. There is so much we know that we won't publish because our obsessive research has led to many discoveries that would be of little interest to readers. What we share is what we know to be useful. This book is something that lies between the simplified and the more esoteric. It is, of course, a book of practical magick. It is not, however, quite as simple as the books that have come before. In some books, it really is a case of *say this, do that*, and *get a result*. But do not worry that this magick will be weird, difficult, or strange. It is not, by any stretch of the imagination, difficult, but it is fair to say that it is not as simple as reading a few words of power and watching things happen.

Why, though, with all that we have published, is there a need for another book? After all, when so much magickal knowledge already exists, are we really suggesting you don't yet have enough tools to create the life you desire? Although we have an enthusiastic audience who ask us to reveal more and more books, there comes a point where you *do* have everything you need to achieve what you want with magick. It could be said, quite reasonably, that by dedicating yourself to the practices that work best for you, there is nothing else you need. It is also true that for some people, one or two books work better than the rest, and so there is always the hope that one more book will reveal something else as powerful.

It should be noted, however, that there are no books that are intrinsically superior. Some people get the most out of *Angels of Alchemy* and *Magickal Servitors*, while others will never use them and stick with *The 72 Angels of Magick*. It is true that some testing and tasting is important to discover what works best for you. And it is also true that what works for you now may change, and an old book that seemed unimpressive at one time can become everything you need.

One reader, on discovering Adam Blackthorne's book *Sigils of Power and Transformation*, announced that this was the only book he would ever need. There was enough magick in there to achieve all that he wanted. And that is fair. This book, though, is more than one more thing to read. It is a culmination of a journey into magick. It will be found by the people who need it, and it will become useful at exactly the right time. You may find that this is the book you have been looking for and that it begins to meet your needs immediately.

Here you will discover a more direct way to manifest results while simultaneously looking beneath the surface of the ordinary world. What that means is that if you wish to discover the great mysteries of life and also solve your problems at will, this magick is what you're looking for. What I hope to present is a system that can be used at whatever level you desire. If you wish only to sample these powers, you can do so with great ease. If you wish to delve deeper, you can do so. It is all about how you engage with the magick and what you desire at any given time. You may read the book with interest and put it aside for a year or a decade, and then find it becomes what you need at a later time in life. Or you may begin at once, knowing that you are ready to welcome a connection to your Angel.

The magick you find here doesn't require faith, belief, or great imagination. What it does require is an open mind. You may have to do things that seem extremely strange, unmagickal, or unimpressive, and that requires a commitment from you. You may be required to be almost childlike in your approach at times. What is challenging for one person will be so easy for another that it appears to be pointless. Be prepared to be pushed out of your comfort zone and remember that pursuing the magick, even when no progress appears to be being made, is the way to make progress.

Given the push-button nature of so much modern magick, making this kind of commitment can be a challenge. If I can do a ritual in five minutes and get what I want, why do something more intense? The answer is that you don't have to. This destiny is on offer, but it is not an obligation. But if you find that you sense its power, and if you get a feeling for how well this could work for you, the journey will be worthwhile.

The Connection

Many people refer to the Holy Guardian Angel as the HGA. I will call it *the Angel*, or *your Angel*, or *your Guardian Angel*. There is no need to be bound by particular phrasing.

The Angel has different names around the world. It's all too easy to fall into the trap of thinking that one Western tradition is The Truth, but there is a whole world of angelic contact from other cultures that can inform and educate us about new ways of making contact.

Complete Contact is my name for what many people have previously called 'Knowledge and Conversation of The Holy Guardian Angel.' That phrase is connected to particular groups and systems, such as The Golden Dawn, a magickal order that had its heyday in the late Nineteenth Century.

The occultist S. L. Mathers, who initially popularized the idea of the Holy Guardian Angel in Western society, is credited with naming the Angel in this way. I think we should note, however, that he and others initially used a more interesting phrase: 'Knowledge *of* and Conversation *with* The Holy Guardian Angel.' Those small differences change the meaning considerably, and this is probably closer to the experience that most people achieve. You gain knowledge *of* your Angel, which means you attain a full awareness *of* the Angel being real and present. You are then able to have a conversation *with* the Angel. In summary, this means you attain a state where you are able to converse with the Angel directly and seek its wisdom and power.

I will refer to 'Knowledge of and Conversation with The Holy Guardian Angel' as Complete Contact. In this book, Complete Contact means the state in which you know your

Angel and can interact with it as a real entity. In many cases, this means seeing and hearing the Angel. For some people, the contact is less visual and more intuitive, but no less real for being so.

Those who have attained a true connection usually keep the details of their experience private, often at the Angel's behest, but it is quite apparent from a few public revelations that what happens is unique for each individual. You are not required to seek a particular experience to prove that your Angel is authentic. Your personal sense of the Angel and its power to protect, guide and empower you, will be evidence enough that you have attained a genuine and effective connection.

The traditional rituals for contacting the Holy Guardian Angel have a reputation for turning your life into a difficult challenge, and I can attest that this was frequently the case, so it is worth asking whether or not this magick is safe. Those old rituals take an enormous amount of time, they are mentally, emotionally, and spiritually demanding, and they can be too disruptive to mesh with the modern world. Many people report that the old ways almost drove them insane. Some people even suggest that's how such rituals work, by taking you to the edge of your sanity and reality. I do not believe you need to suffer or make life so unstable and strange. This book doesn't contain anything as weird as that, and you'll be pleased to know your Angel can be attained peacefully.

The traditional methods also reinforce the false idea that the Angel is hidden, distant, and almost unattainable. I believe this distracts from the most beautiful truth. Your Angel is close to you now, and no drama is required to strengthen the connection. If you become open to this thought, you may already sense the Angel's presence.

The traditional rituals were also distressingly unreliable. Some people want to believe that if you live in a forest for eighteen months, with a perfectly constructed wand and a vat of magick oil, praying every day for hours, and following the ceremonial instructions exactly, that you are guaranteed success. It is not so.

People have failed completely in such circumstances and attempted these lengthy rituals several times over many years. Anecdotally, and from the few published accounts we can refer to, the results were often horribly disappointing. Even those who obtained this style of contact sometimes regarded it as surprisingly optional and mildly disappointing. It does not have to be difficult, and it should never be disappointing.

This book is different from much of what has been written by other people on this subject, and one major difference is that I do not guide you towards a dramatic final ritual. In the older systems, there is usually a final ritual, with a magnificent moment where you summon the Angel, and at that moment, you succeed or fail.

The pressure of that old approach is so intense that many people are overwhelmed when nothing happens, and fool themselves into a madness of false belief. Others are merely shattered by the lack of success after many months of intense struggle. I believe you should approach all stages of the process with less intensity and less pressure, providing *many* opportunities for the Angel to manifest rather than one high-pressure moment. Complete Contact then becomes a reality that is well within reach, and along the way, the power of magick runs more strongly in your life.

Almost any area of occult exploration is laced with controversy, and the Holy Guardian Angel is a subject that brings about posturing and pretence. Some of the loudest opinions come from those who have never even attempted the work, or who lie about their success. I hope and expect that your work with this book will enable you to form opinions that make *you* an authority regarding your reality. The experience you gain from working with this magick will be more important than anybody else's ideas and opinions, including mine. I can shine a light and point you in the right direction, but what you discover will be yours.

The subject of the Angel is a source of great contention, and of all the arguments that occur in occultism, this is often one that brings the most bitterness. Some occultists go so far as to say that anything that strays from the method they have used, even slightly, will fail. You are free to discover that they are wrong.

I find it sad that the quest for this most beautiful experience has led to some fierce and cruel attacks, only because opinions differ. In forums, meetings and correspondence, I have frequently witnessed, or been the subject of messages which say, when paraphrased, 'My Holy Guardian Angel is real and yours isn't.' It reminds me of arguments amongst children about who owns the best toys. As workers of magick, we should rise above this.

Let me make peace here by saying that I accept all other methods that I have read about regarding methods for obtaining Knowledge and Conversation of The Holy Guardian Angel. They all work, and this book is nothing special. But it is an option, and an option that I am sure readers who are familiar with my work will enjoy using. It should present a style of working with magick that presents a sufficient challenge and an immense opportunity, without being too demanding.

What I present here is not the only option, and I will explore the other options to a small degree, so you can take your own path. But even if you choose to use the oldest methods, or the most popular methods, I believe the Protocols included in this book will help your quest immeasurably.

Traditionally, it has required up to eighteen months of dedicated work, withdrawing from life and accepting the turmoil and challenges that arise from the undertaking. That is not the ritual process I describe here, and you can progress without any such turmoil.

I have been hesitant to release this knowledge for several reasons. I believe it is important, but I know it will be rejected by many because it does not echo, mimic, or repeat the practices that have been in place for centuries. I can only accept that some people believe there is only one way. I cannot change those beliefs. So, I put this work out there for people who sense there may be another way.

And you may look at me, and my work, and wonder what right I have to tell you how this should be done. I'm a man who's written books about the magick of seduction and wealth. How can I be the person to guide you on such a deeply spiritual quest? The truth is I have no special place or power granted to me, but I have knowledge, experience, and many decades spent working with people who have taken this journey. I have worked with many of the greatest occultists. What I share here is the work of all those I have known, concentrated into the most efficient of methods.

As for those books about money, sex, and other material desires, I make no excuses. We are humans with material desires, and I believe that using magick to fulfil those desires is one of the fastest ways to increase your spirituality. When you struggle through life without magick, you feel like you are suffering in a dead and unresponsive universe. When you use magick to make life easier and get what you want, you become a part of creation. Ironically, you may become less attached to material goods. The more you get, the less interested you are in obtaining more. And then you find yourself becoming more spiritual without even trying. It's almost impossible to even say what 'spiritual' means, but I will say there is nothing unspiritual about indulging in pleasures. You may be surprised to find that some people even believe the best way to contact the Holy Guardian Angel is through a sexual lust for this 'secret lover.' That's not my approach, but it's a glimpse into the fact that it's all too easy to jump to conclusions when it comes to spirituality.

I loathe greed, and I often work to make things fair for those who are struggling, especially artists, but I openly admit that I like having money, using money, and living a full and sensual life. Being spiritual doesn't mean rejecting the world and looking to the heavens for grace, but embracing the world and the place you choose to be in the world. It's about experiencing reality rather than avoiding reality. And as you do this, the feelings you generate will connect you to your Angel, and the uplifting of the spirit that occurs then is beautiful and true.

I can reassure you that I am not going to make you pray at all. I am not going to put you through intense ceremonies that take hours of heartfelt devotion. Instead, there are a few ways of being that work in combination to bring about contact. The Angel is open to magickal connection in ways that are easier to achieve than people want you to know.

You will use seven Protocols and seven sigils to expand your inner magickal energy and awareness. This awareness is channelled to you through your Angel, helping to strengthen contact. It's easy to miss this point, so I will try to make it clear. When you begin this work, it is not only you that's taking part in the magick. As soon as you begin, the Angel senses your desire for contact and will reach for you, empowering and supporting your efforts.

You may also find that, quite rapidly, the connection will improve your fortune, clarity, and peace. You will sense the meaning and purpose that could make you experience a genuinely fulfilled life.

Your Angel is not hidden behind a veil of occultism. Your Angel is and always has been involved with you and your life. The purpose of the magick is only to raise your awareness of the Angel that is already with you. It is my hope that in working through the magick in this book that you will discover the ease and bliss of opening to your Angel.

Discovering The Angel

You may want to know what the Angel is, what it can do, why you have one, and where all these ideas come from.

At this point, it's worth reflecting on your own beliefs and the feelings that brought you to this book. Is the Angel something you've always believed in, sensed, or in some way experienced? Is it an intuitive feeling, faith, or a sense of truth, or just something you've heard many rumours about? Could it even be the Angel is something you don't actually believe in yet, but wish to explore because of its status in the occult scene? Or do you just like the idea of magick that works?

What I suggest is that you spend some time thinking about why you believe (or don't believe) in a Guardian Angel, what you expect from this book, and why you were drawn to this idea. It doesn't matter what you believe or what you've read before, but spend some time thinking about this before you read on. It's worth examining your beliefs because they are almost certainly going to change.

Too much theory can get in the way of magick, but it helps to know some of the current and historical beliefs about the Angel. Although I will delve into the past in this chapter, I can assure you that every word you read here will help your efforts to contact your Angel.

What I am about to relate is a brief, possibly amusing, almost absurd, and admittedly incomplete history. It might make you wonder why there is so much interest in this subject, but I hope it makes you see that, whatever else goes on, the Angel creates an energy of desire because it is real and because we long to make contact.

The mistakes and missteps of the past make the work easier for us today. There are secrets that emerged from this history, and when deciphered, they can point us in the direction of what is genuine, effective, and true regarding this subject. You may not pick it all up now, but if you read this chapter again in a few years, you may see this history in a new light.

From an early age, I knew that magick was real, but the documents and texts of magick were hidden from me by circumstance. Although I started out with magick at a very young age, crafting my own spells and finding whatever books I could, it was a different era, and it was difficult to find useable methods.

Living in a rural English village in the eighties, the very best library I could access had almost no information, and the bookshops in the nearest town were even worse. The esoteric books (on subjects such as psychic power and astral projection) sat alongside the occasional book of magick theory. You could order practical magick pamphlets through a mail-order service advertised in astrology magazines, but gaining an overview of magick was difficult.

Today, a twelve-year-old can go online and, in a few hours, gain access to more documents regarding the Angel than I could possibly relate in a book ten times the length of this one. What matters is not the information that's available but that you are drawn to seek the Angel. Even though I had little access to magick, I was drawn to the subject of magick, and as soon as I heard of the Angel, it became something that burned at the back of my mind.

Strangely, I think I first heard the phrase 'Holy Guardian Angel' from some Catholic friends. I was from a Church of England school (despite being brought up atheist), and just across the road was a Catholic school. This was common in England, and there was a mild mistrust between those schools (propagated by the parents), but we mixed with all children easily, especially as we grew older and everybody started looking for girlfriends and boyfriends.

I was already working with magick, but I'd debate the nature of religion, spirituality, and the occult for hours with my friends. It was during those talks, especially the less confrontational ones, that I heard the idea that we each had a Guardian Angel, assigned by God, to help us connect with God. In hindsight, I can see that my friends' knowledge and ideas were sometimes far from conventional, but they helped to get me thinking about this idea. I still had no idea that occultists also believed in a Holy Guardian Angel, but now began to sense an important truth. It was *possible* that there was already an Angel with me.

Shortly thereafter, I experienced dreams where I sensed that my Angel was present. These dreams and feelings left me after some weeks, and I put the concept of the Angel aside for a while. There was nothing else to read, do, or attempt at that point.

Like most occultists from that era, my first real brush with detailed theories and ideas about the Angel came through Aleister Crowley's work. You cannot imagine how difficult it was to get hold of Crowley's books in those days, especially if you were a teenager. It took a fair amount of sleuthing to achieve. If I'd lived in London, it would have been much easier, but in the country towns there was ruthless censorship by superstitious adults, and a lack of access to books. Without the internet, it was difficult to find like-minded people, and I hadn't even heard of Crowley until I'd spent several years working with various forms of rustic magick and casual spell-casting.

When I managed to borrow books and pamphlets by Crowley, I didn't understand what I was reading. His works came across as a form of strange poetry, rambling thought, and pompous opinion hidden behind an aloof symbolism rather than any kind of magickal instruction. This almost put me off pursuing magick any further. I was fairly well educated, and having read *Beowulf* and Chaucer, I believed I was at ease with archaic languages. Crowley was something else altogether. His instructions for attaining Knowledge and Conversation of The

Holy Guardian Angel in *Liber Samekh* was far more of a challenge than anything I'd read before.

It felt like his writing was deliberately obscure. It was more like a code than an explanation. I know now that his works rely on your knowledge of other strange texts and symbols. Today, I understand his writing and why he disguised so much (often to avoid persecution), but for a relative beginner, it was a burden of confusion. I was also alarmed that this man, who was apparently the authority on the Holy Guardian Angel, was also regarded by most people as an evil Satanist. It was difficult to ascertain whether this was negative propaganda or true insight into the man.

Following my uneasy reading of *Liber Samekh*, I tried performing his suggested Bornless Ritual several times, but felt as though nothing had happened. That is unsurprising, given my hesitant attitude, but I also discerned that something was not quite right with that ritual. Although it may be useful, and many people say they benefit from its energy, for me, it didn't feel like it had anything to do with the Angel I longed for.

Sometime later, I dared to seek out Crowley's *Goetia*, which was a book for contacting demons. I was baffled to see a variation of the *Liber Samekh* Bornless Ritual in there, but now it was being used as a Preliminary Invocation for contacting demons. What was his ritual, really? Was it for summoning demons or for contacting the Angel? Was Crowley deceptive, or was he recycling familiar rituals for different outcomes? I couldn't be sure, but I was left with the sense that this ritual was probably not the purest way to contact the Angel.

You can unravel the complete history yourself if it interests you, but in modern times we now know that Crowley's *Goetia* was almost like Chaos Magick (where you can make up whatever you want and believe it will work.) It's a mix of concepts and rituals that were often unrelated to the primary sources. The Bornless Ritual, so central to *Liber Samekh*, was a modified exorcism based on workings from the *Greek Magickal Papyri*. It had nothing to do with the Angel at all.

Notwithstanding all these outlandish contradictions and the apparently reckless and hodgepodge nature of Crowley's instruction, many people claimed to have obtained contact with the Angel using his methods. This didn't make much sense to me at the time and I wanted to find another way.

There was hope. I was told that Crowley had based some parts of his work on a text known as *The Abramelin*. That was the original source, and if I wanted the Angel, I needed that book.

Translated by S. L. Mathers, its full title was *The Book of The Sacred Magic of Abramelin The Mage*, and it took me quite some time to get my hands on a copy. It was written in a style that is often compared to that of the King James Bible, which means it felt very old-fashioned and too obscure. And what was I meant to think of the instructions which included using a six-year-old child to assist with the magick? I wanted to contact my Angel, but I wasn't going to procure a child.

The whole idea began to feel ridiculous and sinister. What I read in that book described a six-month process that was anything but straightforward. I began to see why Crowley had made up his own method instead. *The Abramelin* was too weird.

Some occultists insist that *The Abramelin* is the only method that should ever be used to contact the Angel. If you follow it devoutly, they say, then after a certain number of months of magickal work, your Angel appears. When this happens, according to that book, your first task is to bind evil spirits such as Lucifer and Satan. When you've done that, you have the power to work with some magick squares, which supposedly grant you the power to make it snow or turn somebody into an animal. It all sounds outlandish when summarized like that, but I'm not mocking it so much as relating the confusion I felt when contemplating this work.

My personal intuition about the nature of the Angel had a very different quality to this. The Angel I sensed felt like a personal guardian and an expression of magick, not a spirit for binding demons and making snow.

The Book of Abramelin The Mage was originally written by Abraham of Worms in the Fifteenth Century. It tells the story of Abraham seeking out a wise man called Abramelin, who may or may not be fictional, in order to discover magick. The book is about Abraham's attempt to pass magickal knowledge down to his curiously absent son. It was not meant to be read widely, it seems, although others have argued that writing it as a fictional 'message' was an attempt to make it much more widely known. Whatever the truth may be, the book went unnoticed for hundreds of years.

We should recall that Crowley (and many others that came after) believed that the magick squares presented at the end of the book were of the utmost importance. Crowley was awed by them, and didn't hide his fear of their power. Despite this, many people entered into magick during the Twentieth Century precisely because they were lured by the potential power of those legendary squares. It was said that you could wield their power only when you had obtained Knowledge and Conversation of The Holy Guardian Angel.

A multitude of eager occultists approached the Angel as a means of obtaining the power of the squares. There were also many tales of people suffering greatly should they dare to use the magick squares without first completing the six-month *Abramelin* ritual. People were truly terrified of those magick squares.

What nobody knew at the time is that the treasured *Abramelin* was deeply flawed, and the magick squares were so inaccurate that they may as well have been fakes.

Mathers had translated a French text, which was itself a translation of a hopelessly unreliable source. For more than a century, excited occultists had faithfully used a book that was riddled with errors, omissions, additions, and good old-fashioned nonsense. And yet, it worked. This, to me, is the most interesting point. I am not mocking *Abramelin*, or Mather's work (he did his best with what he had), but I am noting that even an utterly bastardized version of the ritual worked for some people.

Does this mean *The Abramelin* is so powerful that even when distorted, it remains effective? That is not how I see it. Let us not forget that when Crowley took this work and attempted to simplify the materials, he created another working that was viewed by some as the only way to contact the Angel. And that method worked as well. Clearly, there are many paths to the same place. I began to suspect that any sincere method could work.

Crowley didn't believe his method was the best or the only way of attaining the Angel. For a change, he was surprisingly modest. Over time I found that he implied in various books and documents that *anybody* could make up their own ritual for attaining contact. This is what I have found to be true because the Angel is a willing participant and does not need to be forced to unite with you more closely.

I am not a great admirer of Crowley. His writings are filled with obsessions, weird combinations of ideas, and many discouraging contradictions. At one point, Crowley said the Angel was the Higher Self. Later, he said that was an abhorrent claim and that the Angel was a real, distinct entity. Despite being regarded as an authority on the subject, he was *significantly* confused about the Angel on many occasions, and struggled to make a satisfying level of contact. But I acknowledge that despite his *many* flaws, he made memorable contributions to popular occultism, not the least of which is showing that you can develop personal magick and get it to work.

What I eventually took from Crowley is that the Angel is yours, and you don't need any ritual to connect with it, but magick can and will aid your efforts to make contact.

So, I moved on, and my work with the Angel was initially based on intuition. Later, I was able to use the methods you find in this book.

In 2001 a new translation of *The Abramelin* appeared, first in German, then a few years later in English, and this clarified what many had suspected. It was clear to see, as mentioned above, that Mathers' *Abramelin* was mostly incorrect.

The new translation, by George Dehn, was based on far more reliable source materials, and many things were now changed or absent. Additional materials were revealed, such as long lists of spells. The magick squares had changed completely. They were so different from those in circulation that it was obvious that the old squares, once so revered, were too corrupt to have ever been effective.

Perhaps the most interesting point to note when reading the new translation is that there is a lot of padding wrapped around a very brief description of the Angel technique. The instructions for the operation of magick are contained in three extremely short chapters. When summarized, the practical chapters of *Abramelin* say you should pray with all your heart for eighteen months. There is not much more instruction than that.

Perhaps the biggest shock was discovering that the ritual was meant to take eighteen months. Everybody who had used the Mathers version found it difficult enough to dedicate themselves to six months.

There are some additional ideas regarding wands and oils, but these appear to have been added at a later time, and they are described as being *unnecessary*. Even the instructions for binding demons are not required; *The Abramelin* acknowledges this with a dismissive phrase, saying the lessons on the subject are as *unnecessary* as the wands and oils.

There's a huge irony here. Many people have used the content of *The Abramelin* to insist that the Angel can only be attained with special oils and by binding demons. When properly translated, *The Abramelin* itself says that none of that stuff matters.

The new translation cleared up many errors, but did little to reveal a pure and appealing method for contacting the Angel. There were a few fascinating ideas that struck me when I read it, and they resonated with what I'd already discovered and experienced, but it was no goldmine. *Abramelin* contains a lot of material that makes no sense today, such as the advice to change your clothes once a week, the recommendation to cease all rituals if you are over fifty, and the rule to keep women away from magick. Ideas like this have long since been abandoned.

Some of the more dogmatic practitioners still believe wands, oils, and demon bindings are what it's all about. When people focus on such details, it's because tinkering with such distractions is a pleasant form of procrastination.

In preparing to write this book, I reread much of what I already knew about the Angel and was astonished at how conservative some people are regarding this subject, even today. There are authors who obtained contact with their Angel using the old and corrupt *Abramelin*, who parade around as though they are in some way superior for having used the 'true' method. They conveniently ignore the new translation, which proves their methods were far from true. These people insist that you will fail unless you do it their way, even though their way was objectively wrong.

I have spoken to occultists who say, 'If you don't use the *Abramelin* method, you may contact *something*, but it will not be your Angel.' This is arrogance and propaganda. It's a way of frightening people, and it is also false. I am aware that it can put doubt in the heart of the vulnerable. You may worry that you might not get the *right* Angel or the *real* Angel. You may even be told that you've made a servitor, which is a sort of temporary spirit created with the imagination. The hoards may attempt to convince you that your Angel is not genuine.

Many ordinary people, who never even practice magick, sense a connection to their Angel at some point, and to dismiss a connection as 'not the real Holy Guardian Angel' is obscene snobbishness. Although there are indeed other helpful spirits in the world, and other guardian spirits, I am bewildered when occultists dismiss the human experience of the Angel as 'unauthentic.'

Many people have sensed their true Angel at some point in their ordinary life. Although this is not the complete level of connection sought through magick, it is real. Your Angel is and always has been involved with you and your life.

Everyday human experience has to be as relevant, if not more relevant, than the writings of haughty occultists. What you experience is real, and you should not let anybody tell you that your discoveries are in any way false.

It may be helpful to recall that many people attempted the *Abramelin* and other methods, several times, without any success at all. Those methods are not foolproof. Crowley himself made quite a few attempts, dismissing his earlier success, trying again and again, as though seeking a better version of the Angel each time. I think that helps give us some perspective and belittles the idea that the old ways are infallible.

Before I knew any of this, I had the fearful belief that only by using quite specific magick rituals could you ever achieve contact with the Angel. Later, when I was traveling in my twenties, I saw from the varied spiritual traditions of the world that this could not be true. I met many people who achieved contact with the Angel using their own methods, arising from their religious and cultural practices. There were varying degrees to which this contact was achieved and various beliefs about the nature and purpose of the Angel, but the Angel was real to more people than I could have imagined.

Cynics might say these cultures were not connecting with the Angel, but that is insulting. All over the world, people have found ways to connect with their Angel. Those connections are valid.

As I have already implied, you will find, if you read more widely, that many people have extreme opinions about the Angel, and some write angrily, as though doing so will prove a point. For such an illuminating and beautiful subject, this is quite baffling. My impression of those who write so angrily about the Angel is that whatever process they used doesn't seem to have done them much good because they insist, 'I have my Angel and nobody else does.' They write surprisingly vicious diatribes on all manner of theories. People who are at peace with the presence of the Angel don't need to get so riled up. I hope you find this book gentle and not too opinionated. I would never want to be one of those writers who is frothing at the mouth.

I believe we are all assigned an Angel, and far from being remote from us, it is intimately connected to us whether we perform magick or not. When we do perform magick, we become closer to the Angel. When we are afraid, inspired, or in love, we are closer to the Angel. When we seek contact with the Angel, the contact is there immediately, and then, when we have the intention to clarify the contact, it becomes more apparent.

I am offering an alternative to the methods that have been previously published, and the magickal Protocols will bring you closer to your Angel. I am not dismissing other methods, but warning against the emphasis on a climactic grand ritual in which the Angel *must* appear. That sort of desperate magick can lead to problems. If you spend a year and a half meditating in isolation, praying your way to the Angel, then performing a grand finale, the lack of results can be unbearable. Or the need to play out this huge revelatory moment may lead to self-deception.

There is something cult-like about the idea that reaching for the Angel must be a trial. The Protocols described here allow you to reach for your Angel without destroying your world or your mind. You should find that the Angel brings peace and purpose quite rapidly, and if that is far from traditional, I am glad. Although it may not be that far from tradition because even the *Abramelin* states that soon after you begin, the Angel will stand by your side and guide you through the process. Which goes to show that the traditions of the past have been needlessly twisted into a process far more harrowing than it ever needed to be. It will not be that way for you.

Your experience of the Angel, even if you throw this book away and follow *Abramelin* to the letter for eighteen months, may not be what you expect. I think back to what Crowley said about how different people experience the Angel. He was quite right in saying that people with strong visual abilities will eventually see the Angel, people who favour sounds may hear music, and those whose minds are less imaginative won't experience more than a sense of a presence. Imagination does not create the Angel, but a strong imagination can clarify your perception of the Angel.

If your imagination is poor, your Angel will be present but in a less concrete way, and that will be acceptable. For many people, there may never be a dramatic moment of visual revelation, and it's important to be upfront about that. A slow-burning relationship, where it feels that your Angel is always with you (because it always has been and always will be), is better than the pressure of trying to make it appear in front of you at all costs. If you are not imaginative, you may only sense your Angel, and no amount of magick will cause a full and physical manifestation. You will find that this is absolutely satisfactory because your personal connection will be exhilarating and empowering, whatever the form it takes.

This history I have skimmed over here is only part of one history. There are other stories, some relating to Greek texts, and others claiming to be from even further back. As mentioned, if you travel widely, you find that for every culture, there is a story that includes the Angel. What we have in the West is only a splinter of the light, and we are free to work with what has gone before or discover new ways of finding the Angel.

Having come this far, you have options. You may choose to work with Dehn's *Abramelin* or Crowley's *Liber Samekh*, although that's clearly not what I recommend. You may attempt to invent your own methods, and that can work. If you like what you find in this book, I recommend using the Protocols revealed here to obtain bliss, and to experience a connection to your Angel.

Although occultists have wrapped themselves up in knots over this subject, the Angel is real and readily accessible using any method you desire. And it's all so much easier than people would have you believe.

The Reality of Contact

One of the most inescapable topics is whether the Angel is your higher self, your future self, an aspect of your inner self, a separate entity, or something else not yet explained. There are two primary beliefs, with some who believe the Angel is a form of your higher self, and others convinced the Angel is a spirit that exists independently from you while being intimately connected to you.

In practice, you do not need to form a concrete belief before you experience the Angel, and contact is more convincing than any description or expectation. Earlier, you were guided to consider your current thoughts on the Angel, but note that your beliefs can be flexible and will probably evolve as you obtain contact.

You will almost certainly find that the Angel is not a 'magickal friend' that gives you gossipy advice. But it is not a being so lofty that it will attempt to sway you from a life of pleasure and success. The Angel wants you to succeed in a way that feels right to you, so you are content when you want to be, or striving with confidence when you aim to achieve more.

I have resisted the temptation to suggest that your Angel can make you rich, happy, and completely at peace. My belief is that a life with your Angel is always better than it would be otherwise, but that does not mean everyday reality is set aside.

A non-magickal life can be a struggle. You strain to reach your dreams and goals, swayed by the chaotic choices of millions of other people. Seeing your efforts bear fruit is more about random luck than intention. With magick, you choose to take more control over how the events of your life unfold.

You may already work with magick to cause such effects, and if you do, working with your Angel will unlock the power of that magick in ways you could never have dreamed of before. You will become aware of what you want, what will benefit you the most, sensing how and when to use the magick you know, while being guided to seek magick that could take you deeper.

If you do not use magick yet, working with the Angel might lead you to seek out magickal techniques, but you are not required to use other magick. With this book and the Angel's guidance, you may find that this is all you need to achieve an effective life.

A connection with the Angel means you will find that simple acts of desire and decision can make things happen. Magick becomes a part of who you are, and magick happens without you even having to perform rituals. I am not saying this will happen overnight, but as you become familiar with the Angel, you will begin to make things happen with ease.

This point should not be underestimated. Many readers assume that members of The Gallery of Magick must be casting spells and performing rituals every day, but that is not true. Although we use magick with great purpose and ambition, we also know that the more powerful you become, the *less* magick you perform. As you become at one with the powers of magick, the less magick you *need* to perform. Using the methods in this book will guide you toward this state.

This doesn't mean your life becomes free of all errors and accidents or that you can wish for instant success. But the balance of power will be in your favour. When you are working with magickal purpose, reality responds, and even your casual wishes begin to come true.

I will not offer further instruction on this aspect of the book at this point because everybody has a different pathway through magick. But I can assure you that if you make the methods in this book a part of your life, you will begin to understand what I mean. And you will see magickal results manifesting without any more effort than a simple decision or desire. As your connection to your Angel grows, magick will keep unfolding and expanding for you.

To begin with, you should not focus on this aspect of the work, but know that it is possible. To get underway, read thoroughly, use the Protocols as described, connect with the Angel, and notice how manifestation becomes a part of the way you live.

I think some people expect the Angel to be a solution to all problems, and that with an Angel by your side, everything will surely be alright. It isn't quite like that. When you are closer to your Angel, life will be better, magick will be easier, and factors such as luck and coincidence will work in your favour, and every problem will carry within it a secret benefit. Always look for that benefit. But also accept that life is never going to be cushions and silk. That is good because we all enjoy the flow of moving powerfully past problems.

If anybody promises that the Angel will make life so easy that you never have to worry again, they are lying to you, and I will not take part in such deception. If you are willing, you can look beyond false promises and allow the truth of this magick to work with you and through you, bringing results and benefits that outweigh any expectations.

While this truth may seem to contradict what I said earlier about problems solving themselves, there is no contradiction. It is true that life will remain filled with challenges and surprises, but it is also true that you will develop the ability to manifest magickal results at will. These truths are more compatible than they may first appear.

You may wonder if you will become spiritually strange and obsessive, or in some way bound to do the bidding of your Angel. This cannot happen. The Angel will never force you to do anything or try to change who you are. It may encourage you down paths that you never knew you were able to locate, or down paths that were once too challenging for you, but you are the one who chooses where to go.

It has already been noted that the traditional focus is on contacting your Angel to deepen a connection with God, and I know that many people would prefer to use ritual magick without any trace of religion. Although work that involves divinity may be acceptable or even enticing to some readers, many people want their Angel, but they do not want God. They have been so disillusioned by dogmatic religion that they don't even believe in any conventional God. I was brought up atheist, and yet I wanted to know my Angel, so I understand how this can feel. Let me put your mind at rest. Although the spiritual journey toward a higher power is real, the Angel guides you to become an active and important part of reality, to create your life in accordance with your true needs and (often hidden) abilities. This is far from being stuck in a Sunday School class.

What's truly at play here is not religion or belief, but commitment to intention. No amount of sugar-coating can hide the fact that Complete Contact takes time. People want books where you say four magick words and get a result in seconds because anything else is too difficult. I understand that the ease of some Gallery of Magick books has contributed to this trend, but I do not believe magick should always be simplified and shrunk. If you take too much away, there may be nothing left other than wishful thinking and confirmation bias.

I hope you go into this work with a genuine desire to seek contact rather than to prove something to other people. We often hear claims that connection to the Angel has made somebody Adept, or has initiated them into some new magickal order, or that they have achieved a special magickal grade. These labels are no more impressive than cheap trophies for minor accomplishments. The Angel is for *you*, and with a genuine connection, there is no need to brag or make claims about how powerful you are. Be wary of all who claim such authority.

The magick of the Angel is safe. Sometimes people buy a text of magickal instruction, and within a few days, they suffer an accident, or something unusual happens, such as a bird flying into the bedroom window. Sometimes something worse happens, such as a more serious accident or the arrival of an unexpected expense. If something like this occurs, do not be discouraged, but understand that ordinary accidents and occurrences will not dry up when you reach for your Angel. Your life has always been filled with strange occurrences and unlucky moments. If they befall you now, they are *ordinary* and have *not* been caused by magick.

I will also say that if something wondrously good happens, it was probably going to happen anyway, and it would be poor taste to suggest that good fortune was caused by your new book of Guardian Angel magick. Good things happen, and bad things happen, and the Angel's influence on your reality will be gradual. You can safely dismiss extremes of experience in the early days of working with the magick, and you can be certain that misfortune is never caused by your attempt to reach the Angel.

Although this knowledge is a useful way to ground yourself, you should become open to identifying moments when your connection to the Angel becomes stronger. Like many aspects of magick, this may seem contradictory, but it is not. If you remain open to the Angel, you might find that the Angel finds a way to make itself known. It might be a sensation, a strange feeling, a sweet-smelling breeze, or the way the light glitters on the water. *Something* will make you feel that the Angel is with you.

It may be that a pattern of coincidence occurs, and it becomes evident that something extraordinary is happening to you. You may start the Protocols, and ten minutes later, you hear somebody talking about their Guardian Angel, or you may see a white bird or something else that feels symbolic of your Angel. Trust these moments and the feelings they bring.

If you remain open, you'll probably experience something like this within the first days or weeks. Do not yearn for these revelations or clues, but when they happen, know that the Angel is communicating with you. Acknowledge that you have begun something important, and know that the contact is real.

The experience of the Angel is so varied that describing it is fruitless, but you should remain open to sensing the Angel's presence. I do not need to state this too explicitly, as many of the practices that follow are designed to enable your opening up to the reality of the Angel.

Be prepared for any level of contact that may occur. Earlier, I spoke of the traditional rituals, where the Angel is summoned to appear before you, as a real and tangible being. Although I have made it clear that the pressure of those rituals is impractical, more dramatic forms of contact are possible. While it is more likely that initial contact will be subtle, and even Complete Contact can occur in gentle and intuitive ways, the methods in this book do lead to the most intense and stunning forms of contact at times. You cannot and should not force these moments to happen, but they do happen and can help to cement your rapport with the Angel. So, allow the work to be subtle, and if it becomes more intense, know that is also to be expected for many people.

This magick can remove so many locks, and release so much inner truth, that some people have magnificent experiences in the first week, but be comfortable with your journey even if it takes much longer to notice even the slightest effect. Worrying about your progress will never help, while commitment to the workings will. Keep going and know that these methods for reaching for your Angel cannot invite trouble and will always succeed to some degree. With persistence, they are a pathway to Complete Contact.

The Reality of Doubt

I once saw a brilliant card trick on TV, and I was so baffled that I just had to know how it was done. I'd only ever been interested in occult magick and had little interest in magic tricks, illusions, or conjuring, but this card trick caught my attention. I went into London, tracked down a place that sounded promising, and found myself in a tiny cave-like shop with barely room to stand. The scruffy man selling the instruction books and gimmicks knew what I was talking about. He slapped down a plastic package that contained a miniature booklet and a deck of cards. I paid the money and stood outside the shop, reading the instructions.

A minute later, I felt like I'd really been duped. I'd wasted money on a secret that I should have been able to guess. I was annoyed at myself for ever having been fooled. The idea was too simple.

I went home, and even though I was skeptical that it would be worth the effort, I learned how to do the trick. I performed it as well as I could for my girlfriend, and she had the most amazing reaction. To her, it looked as good as professional magic. The secret was quite basic and easy to do. When performed properly, it looked miraculous.

I was pleasantly surprised, but also puzzled. With just an hour of practice in front of a mirror, the magic looked as good as it had looked on TV. It didn't matter that the secret was simple. It worked. I still do that trick now, every once in a while, thirty-odd years later, and it works.

What I've found is that it's the same with occult magick. If a method is so simple that you find yourself shaking your head and going, 'Oh come on, that will never work,' that's exactly when it will work.

Subtle methods are often the strongest. They remain quite secret without occultists ever having to hide them because they seem to be insignificant. Even when published in relatively popular books, these methods are easily dismissed and quickly forgotten, or assumed to be something quite ordinary. Several of these Protocols may be similar to methods you have seen elsewhere, and many of the authors who share them have no idea these are aspects of magick. In this sense, most of what I present to you here is not new, but it may be secret because it is widely ignored and its magickal potential so misunderstood. You access the secrets by choosing not to ignore these ideas.

What you find in this book will often be so simple and maybe even so obvious that you could dismiss it as being too ordinary. The experience of doubt is almost certain to be a challenge that you will have to overcome as part of this process.

In some ways, this is the easiest magick you will ever find. It may appear insubstantial, lacking in spectacle, and not what you expect. Keep in mind why you are doing this and what a significant breakthrough it will be to know your Angel.

The way into this magick is to find the wonder, eager to discover the depth in these concepts and methods, and to know that greatness is available to you.

I urge you to have the courage to put judgement aside. You are free to judge me and this book, of course, but if you decide to use the magick, use the methods as though you believe they are valid. The act of working with the magick, and believing that it *is* magick, is one of the most powerful commitments you can make.

As mentioned earlier, there's an old myth about working with the Holy Guardian Angel, where people say that as soon as you begin the work, your life falls apart. The myth is powerful and frightening, and that's the reason it gets repeated often. Spreading stories must be fun for some people. But I wouldn't waste your time, or mine, by writing this book if there was a grain of truth in that.

Having guided people through this work, I have *never* seen a slither of evidence for the Angel causing disruption. It's true that when you do this work, you are woken from the slumber of your ordinary life, you see things in a new way, and often, you decide to make changes. The person you are now may well be stripped away to reveal your truth, but there is no magick in this book that is designed to destroy or harm you. And there is *never* an outside force that brings disruption upon you. The Angel will never throw tests or challenges at you as some sort of trial. It will be a spiritual journey, but not one that dismantles you or your life.

The only real disruption I have seen comes from other people telling you that you're doing the work incorrectly, that your Angel is not real, and that you are wasting your time. Beloved partners, friends, occult colleagues, and outsiders may not be as supportive of your efforts as you want them to be. If you have a strong enough sense of self and feel confident in your magickal work, this will hardly bother you. But I have seen some people give up the work because people on the outside try to convince them that this magick is not real.

Again, I do not think this is caused by the Angel or by any supernatural force. It happens purely because the subject is controversial, and many people have dogmatic opinions. If you do the work and enjoy it, other people may feel threatened by your confidence.

You can choose to perform the work in secret. When you keep these experiences to yourself, the connection feels like something that is yours alone, rather than something that is being critiqued by others. There is intimacy in secrecy.

There are many ways to discover the truth of the Angel, and you are free to discover whatever you wish. You are almost certain to experience doubt as you work through this magick, and dealing with your own doubts is healthy and productive. Defending yourself against the doubts of others is a debilitating waste of energy.

Earlier in the book, I noted that the infamous *Abramelin* technique could be crudely summarized as 'pray with all your heart for eighteen months.' I can see that the instructions in this book could be treated the same way and summarized as 'reach for the Angel and see what happens.' If you deconstruct the method, it looks like nothing much at all, and that could be enough to make anybody have doubts.

Some years ago, I wondered if there was a way around this and developed a system using a complex sequence of Angelic sigils to provide a sturdier method that felt more real. It did work. But as a colleague of mine said, you could worship a twig for twelve months, and if you did it with the intention of contacting the Angel, it would work. So, although that method worked, it was too complicated, and the only benefit was that it looked like 'real magick,' which made it easier for people to take it seriously. But I can't bring myself to stuff this book with methods you don't need.

It is almost unheard of for somebody to undertake this work without experiencing doubt. The magick seems too easy, or maybe too abstract, or not powerful enough, or you feel like you should be doing something better with your time. I do not believe that doubt is a necessary part of the work but an inevitable one. There is often quite deep resistance. But when you do the work, there should and will be signs of contact.

When I have taught people directly, and even when using an early version of this book with volunteers, I found that students were quite unwilling to accept this vagueness. They wanted to know what the experience of the Angel would be like, in detail, so they could know what to look for. Is it a giant glowing humanoid with wings, or a voice, or a light, or is it something you sense through intuition, synchronicity, and things that happen in your life? Can you actually talk to it and get answers? Does it always look the same to you, or will it evolve? Does it invoke awe, fear, or love? And along with those questions, hundreds of similar ones. All of which are fair enough. As one person pointed out, it's difficult to reach for the Angel or try to sense its presence if you have no idea what you're reaching for. This thought also worried some students who thought that they might reach for the wrong entity.

These are all reasonable concerns, but as for safety, there is no issue. The Angel knows you are seeking contact and protects you. There is nothing else you need to do. As for knowing what the Angel is meant to be like, it is impossible to answer because no two experiences are alike, and when people feel permitted to explain the experience, they struggle to find adequate words. Your perception of the Angel can certainly evolve and change over time, and it's true that sensing the Angel can range from noticing changes in your life to feeling a conscious presence, right through to seeing and knowing a being as though it were physically present with you. But you do not need a preconception of the Angel in order to seek the Angel. You have read enough here, and contemplated enough yourself, that when you seek the Angel, you cannot fail but to catch its attention.

The Angel is not concealed and is never absent or remote. It is only distant from your consciousness because of the state you are in at any given moment. With the smallest, easiest of methods, you can make contact. Becoming aware of this can be the first step to fully connecting with your Angel.

Any time you sense the Angel, treasure the moment, hold onto that memory, and let the Angel lead you through all periods of doubt. Commit to performing the magick, knowing that at some point, there will be an undeniable sign that you are on the right path. It may take weeks or months, or you may feel something hours, minutes, or moments from now.

The Role of Intention

By now, you probably want to get on with the magick, but if you're feeling impatient, remember that I'm not sending you out to build a shelter in the forest, while creating complex oils and giving up your old existence for months. By comparison, what follows is relatively easy.

I understand that the urge to start doing something is strong, and that's good, but you *are* doing something by reading these words. It's an important part of the process. What you take in now will feed and inform your progress. And how you respond to the ideas in this chapter is as important as anything else.

For many years, people have asked me about the best way to contact their Angel. One of the most rewarding things I have ever done is to help people attain that contact. And having helped so many people, I've been able to get a lot of insight into how people approach this challenge. When people ask me how to contact the Angel, the first question I now ask in return is, 'What have you already tried?' This question makes some people look at me blankly. Their answer, when they eventually find the words, is that they haven't tried anything because they were looking for the right method. In response to that, I always say, you might be surprised what happens if you just try. No instruction, no technique; just try.

Other people who are seeking the Angel tell me they have tried all sorts of techniques and traditional methods, of course, and many have grown frustrated with the effort. But most have tried nothing.

It makes sense. You can't learn to fly a plane until you can afford flying lessons, hire a plane, and get help from a good instructor. You wouldn't get into the cockpit of a plane and try to make it up to the clouds without some guidance. We can learn through play, experimentation, and adventuring, but mostly we wait for a teacher, a method, a course, a set of rules, and the reassurance that we're learning in the right way. And that is why so many people assume there's no point in doing anything to seek the Angel until they have the right method, the right equipment, and the right instruction. But finding the Angel does not require special equipment, or even an instructor. As I've said, you don't even need this book, but I believe it can help by guiding you to see what you already know, and what you are already capable of achieving.

If I want something as ordinary as a bagel, I will go out and get one. It's no great act of willpower or intention. I just decide to get one. It's easy. Sometimes, though, it's not so easy. If I'm in the wilderness, I'll have to make do with what I have in my backpack, and that's ok, the bagel can wait. But what happens with the Angel is that people assume they are always in the wilderness. They assume they are so far from the reality of the Angel that something else needs to happen first. Nothing else needs to happen.

I've visited several countries where it's difficult to find clean, running water. Places like that change the way you feel about water forever. At home, if I want a clean glass of water, the smallest intention will allow me to have clean drinking water. I expect it to be there. I assume it will be there. The cost is so low that I think of it as being free. Water is just there and I don't have to do much at all to get a glassful. I can even swim in a pool full of clean water. Water is so readily available that I assume it will always be there without any fear or doubt. And this is how it can be with the Angel. You are not shielded from the Angel by a mass of difficult circumstances. You do not have to solve puzzles and meet challenges. The Angel is alongside you now. The Angel is not impossible.

To take the analogy further, I can remember a time when I was traveling alone in a remote part of a country I'd never visited before. I didn't know the language, and due to a brief but intense illness, I'd been unable to buy food or water to keep me going. It took all the energy I had to get into a polluted taxi and travel through the dead of night until I found accommodation. The place I stayed was so rundown that I wouldn't call it a hotel, but it had a bed, and that was what I needed most. Food and water could wait, but not for long. Looking out of the tiny window, I couldn't see anywhere that looked like it might sell food. I became anxious.

Although quite young at the time, I had already travelled enough to know that if there are people around, there are ways to find food and water, even if it takes some effort to communicate, and some bartering. But I was weak from the illness, and couldn't imagine trekking around town. I struggled my way through the night with little sleep, feeling dehydrated and apprehensive.

In the morning, I made my way outside, and the view was just as disappointing in daylight. Until I turned around. Behind me, there was a bustling marketplace, with so much food and drink that I could have feasted indefinitely. I should have trusted what I already knew. People cannot survive without an infrastructure that provides food and water. Where there are people, there will be food and water. I knew that, and I should have trusted that and slept peacefully.

And this is how it is with the Angel. Right now, you may feel like the Angel is remote, distant, hard to reach, and you may feel that you will have to wander, search, bargain, and deal your way to the Angel. But in truth, you might only need to look in a slightly different direction. You can do this with the act of intention. When you intend to know your Angel, you are heard, and the contact begins.

And so, I always ask would-be students what they have done so far. It's a way of making you see that until you try something, nothing happens. And when you try, you may be surprised at what you are able to achieve.

I completely understand the problem people face. It's reasonable to assume that new skills take time to learn. If you pick up a basketball for the first time and try to get it through that hoop, you *might* succeed. But it will probably take longer. You might even find it so difficult that you begin to doubt yourself. You might even give up. If you don't give up, you'll find that getting it through the hoop more often than not takes committed, daily practice.

This is true for almost everything we do, from cooking dinner to driving a car, to learning the skills needed for a career, or mastering a hobby. We come to take these skills for granted, but they are often difficult to acquire. Some things come more naturally than others, but even when a skill feels natural, it still needs to be practiced. So, it's easy to assume that the magickal techniques required for Angelic connection are going to be the same.

The mistake we make is assuming that contacting the Angel is a skill, like learning to juggle or read music. The reality of contact is not about acquiring skills or doing new things, so much as directing your intention and then allowing contact. When you intend to contact the Angel, almost everything you do will help you to attain contact. Making an active intention to contact your Angel, using *any* method – even one you invent – can work effectively. The intention to make contact makes contact happen.

Many people resist this idea, thinking there must be a secret way to unlock the Angel. Although many powerful methods are used later in the book, tapping into secret magick through the use of sigils, it's vital to know that any method can work.

Intention is a curious word. If you intend to do something, that means you are doing more than hoping and wishing. If you intend to open a door, it means you are going to reach out, turn the handle, and open the door. You don't sit there thinking about it or hoping somebody else will open it for you. Intention means you open the door.

If the door is locked, you don't give up. You intend to open the door, so you find the key. If there's no key, it gets a little more complicated. How much do you want to get to the other side? If your intention is firm, you might be willing to pick the lock or break down the door. You might even find another way into that room. Or you might decide that, despite your intention, you can wait. But if the house is on fire and somebody is trapped inside that room, you'll definitely break down the door.

And this is why intention is a curious word. So much depends on how strongly you intend. It's not like an on/off switch, where you either intend or you don't. There are degrees of intention. Sometimes, the word intention can be used as an excuse for something you failed to do. You may say, 'I intended to come to your party but couldn't make it.' That is the sort of intention you want to avoid.

It's important to take a look at these grades of intention, so you know what I mean by the word. In the context of this book, intention is not a weak possibility. It is not a hope or a wish, and certainly not an excuse. Intention is clear. This doesn't mean it takes immense effort, willpower, or unwavering commitment, but it does require a decision. Using the above example, you are not trying to break down the door out of desperation. You know the door is already unlocked, and you are reaching for the handle, turning it, opening the door, knowing it will open.

You intend to do something, and so you will. You intend to contact your Angel, and so you make contact.

If you've got to this point in the book and you feel bewildered or confused because you have already tried to contact the Angel with great intention, what you're reading here may sound like nothing new. It may even sound incorrect because you have tried so hard before. Should that be the case, let me reassure you that this *will* be different because of the way everything has been constructed. Remain open to the possibility of success even if you feel skeptical. I expect that you will be pleasantly surprised by the results you experience.

If, like most people, you have never tried to reach for the Angel in any way, the same advice applies. Don't force yourself to believe anything, but be willing to accept the possibility that this might work.

The practical methods explored in the rest of the book are ways of actively expressing your intention to contact the Angel. When you combine these intentions with openness, magick can occur.

After such a long discourse on intention, you might think this is all very obvious, but examining the role of intention is important, and that should become clear when you explore the following Protocols in practice. They are always an intentional act of contact.

Some people have likened contact with the Angel to a love affair. When you are deeply in love, you are aware of your love (and the one you love) every moment of the day. Whether you are going out for a walk, trying to work, or talking with friends, the power of that new love is always with you, influencing all your thoughts and decisions. You would never go two or three days without thinking about your love. It is always at the forefront of your mind. And to some extent, it can be like this with the Angel, especially in the later stages, but this never has to be forced or sought out. You don't have to become obsessive, or lust and yearn after your Angel.

All that's required is for you to enact some form of intention to make contact, every day if you can. If you miss a day, the Angel won't abandon you, but it's true that consistent attention will render more positive results than something patchier. Even if you miss a day, spare a moment to remember that it is your intention to connect with the Angel.

The techniques and Protocols you find in the book will all employ intention at some level. It is worth noting that magickal intention does have a different quality to everyday intention, in that magickal intention alone can change reality. In ordinary terms, if you walk for an hour every day, your fitness will improve by a certain level. It doesn't matter whether your intention was to get fit, to get to work, or to enjoy the walk. Whatever your intention, you achieve the same level of fitness from all that walking. With magick, your intention changes reality itself. Let's say you go for a walk and your intention is for every step to increase the power of a magickal effect; your intention will make it so. An ordinary walk becomes a magickal act. You will make use of intention in many similar ways as you work with the methods described here.

Don't worry if the role of intention seems like an overload of information at this point. The practicalities will become clear as you begin using the ideas and Protocols to attain contact with the Angel.

Receiving The Angel

When you work with the Protocols and methods as instructed, what actually happens? For some people, there will be an immediate and deeply emotional connection. For some, there will be a few strange tingles and sensations, and that's a great sign. For most people, there may be little or nothing at all, and that is fine.

How can I say it's fine for it not to work? I say this because every attempt does more magickal work than you may ever realise. Each attempt is an act of progression, whether you sense it or not.

Imagine you're trying to shatter a huge block of marble with a small hammer. It might take a thousand blows before it breaks. And until that moment, you might feel like you're making almost no progress because there are only tiny dents on the surface. But every blow of the hammer is shuddering through the entire block of marble, weakening the structure, preparing it for the moment of collapse. Eventually, one more tap will make it shatter. Your magick will always make a difference, even if it is unseen, even when you feel like you are barely denting the surface.

Making the attempt, even if nothing seems to happen, *does* make something happen. Every time you attempt to reach out to the Angel, you are drawn closer to a conscious awareness of its reality.

Be prepared for the fact that you may obtain a strong and immediate response on your first attempt. This can happen because there is nothing external holding the Angel away from you, and when your intention is clear, the connection can be immediate. In fact, it always will be immediate; it's just a case of whether or not you perceive the connection.

If you do experience something, you will probably counter it with doubt. If the Angel speaks, and you hear its voice, you may dismiss this as an illusion, or just your own thoughts. Do not work too hard to determine the reality of what you sense. Only notice what's happening. Using the magick you find here, it does not take too much time for you to clarify the difference between your own thoughts and those that emerge from the Angel.

Be aware that any response may come at a much later time, when you're not even thinking about the Angel. When performing the Protocols, seek the Angel with great intention, but when they are over, be passive, and allow the Angel to make itself known when it will.

The Protocols and energy-raising rituals are the active part of the process, and the passive aspect of this process is to become receptive, to enter a state of allowing. I think this is the reason people used to go out to the forest to do this work. There just aren't as many distractions out there, if you're lucky. But I once worked with a student in Manhattan who said her life never slowed down and was never quiet, even at night. She managed to find a way to be receptive, to reach a state of allowing, and everything worked out fine. Wherever you are, you can do what's required. You don't need to disappear into the woods, but you do need to become open to the world and make space for some peace. This is much easier than it sounds, even if the world around you never slows down or becomes still.

Many people have referred to 'turning down the volume' of life, but that makes it sound like you can never go to parties, or have fun, or seek out all those delightful pleasures that bring you so much happiness. Thankfully, it doesn't have to be like that at all. You are not going to become an ascetic, hiding away, with no social life and no enjoyment. As I said earlier, the point of this work is to bring the Angel into your life more consciously, not to abandon your life. You may, however, need to modify your life a little, so there is more time and space in which contact can be made. In moments of quiet and silence, the most powerful contact is often made. But for some people, the breakthroughs can happen when they are creating music, for example. What then, is required of you?

Have you ever had a conversation where the other person just keeps talking over you? Even when they ask you a question, you don't get a chance to answer because they talk and talk and you never get to speak. When you do manage to find a moment to speak, you can tell that the other person is just waiting for their turn to talk again. This is not a good way to communicate.

When you ask a question, you should wait for a response, and listen to the answer that is given. That opens the way to effective communication. This is also how you work with the Angel. The Protocols are a way of asking for the Angel, and you then need to listen for a response.

Many techniques have been suggested for achieving a state that is akin to listening. These range from various forms of meditation through to trance-like states. If you are into that sort of thing, it can work, but I don't think it's required at all. The approach I suggest is more about remaining open to the possibility that your Angel may make itself known. I think of this as a sort of passive attention. When the Protocols are over, you don't need to deliberately look for signs or reach and strain for something to happen. There is, however, a useful way to remain open to the Angel, and that is to look for beauty in whatever form you can. If you have read our other books, we often talk of a Daily Practice, where you seek beauty even if you are in a place that is not obviously beautiful.

This doesn't have to be a practice that you do deliberately, but a way of being that you bring into your life. When you are in the world, look for beauty, and this will make you so much more receptive to the Angel's communication. It's easy to miss the value of this advice but it is an essential part of the process. You may sense the Angel when engaging in this receptive state, but it may come at another time; what matters is that by opening to beauty more often, you make way for the Angel's power and presence.

You might sense your Angel while out for a walk, or when stacking the dishwasher, or when taking a shower. The mundane is where we live most of the time, so be prepared for magick to intrude on those ordinary moments of existence.

The challenge is to allow yourself to find the time to see beauty, and it's never been more challenging than today. In so many cases, moments are now filled with more distractions; a podcast while you're walking, an audiobook while you're driving, information, news, and entertainment whenever there's a moment of stillness. There's nothing wrong with these things in themselves, but what's wrong is that they have invaded *all* our quiet moments. If you're standing in a queue, sitting in a waiting room, or travelling on a train, it's almost impossible to resist the urge to get out a device and find some information or diversion. Do not be afraid of these still moments. Fill them with beauty by observing, as described. Even if it seems boring, allow yourself to be where you are without seeking anything else than the world around you.

I get a lot of kickback when I suggest this. Nobody wants to give up their phone or cut off from the modern world. Me included. I have two smartphones and two iPads, so I'm not here to say you should get rid of your devices. And please know that it really isn't about the technology at all. I worked with one student, an avid lover of the arts, who was always out watching a play, going to the opera, reading a book, or discussing theatre and art with her friends. She thought that my advice to find quiet time to observe beauty had nothing to do with her because she was always seeing beauty in the arts. But after working with her for a while, it became clear that she was so busy with everything else, her mind was never free; in those ordinary moments, she never noticed the simple beauty of the world around her. Her mind was always racing with stories and reviews and opinions. Again, this is not a criticism of her lifestyle (which was similar to my own at the time), but a clue about how this can work. You don't have to abandon the entertainment you love, but if you can't find even a few moments to notice the world around you, how will you ever notice the Angel that is with you? Open to beauty, and you allow the Angel to be with you.

And when I say you should seek silence or quiet, this does not mean trying to control or silence your thoughts. It only means that you look outwards at the world, without judgment. You observe people, the light, the textures, shapes, and colours. Look at the world as though it is a blessing and a mystery. By looking outward, your inner life ignites. When you accept that the world is beautiful, no matter how ordinary or ugly it seems, you enter a state of allowing. It is in these moments of observation and moments of quiet, where the Angel will be heard, and sometimes, even seen.

Does this mean, then, that the old methods were right, and that it would be wise to disappear to the forest for a few months, without a Wi-Fi connection? I don't think so. You only need to make a few small adjustments. I'm not asking you to throw away your phone and pretend the internet doesn't exist. I am only suggesting that in the quiet, you can open your senses without judgement. That's what brings you into the world. And when you're in the world, you can change it.

I love shallow entertainment as much as the next person. I could watch videos of people landing aeroplanes at different airports for hours. And sometimes I do. But I think everybody knows the difference between something that makes you feel enriched, and something that makes you feel spent. I'm not moralising or being snobby. It's about whether something gives you life or takes it away from you. The clock is ticking, and when you hit fifty, by god, you want to make the most of your time. Some activities seem rewarding, but when you indulge in them too much, they consume you far more than you consume them.

This chapter has hinted, quite strongly, that you should seek out moments of peace and beauty in your ordinary life. There is no technique to be used. All you do is notice there is space that could be filled with an activity or distraction, and instead of filling that space, you leave it empty and observe what is in front of you, and see its beauty. Look at the world and see what you notice. You are not waiting for or expecting the Angel. You are only getting into the habit of allowing a moment of quiet observation. Things may happen. You may sense something. Or nothing may happen at all. But never give up these moments of peace as they are an essential part of the process.

The Seven Protocols

The magick methods that follow are called Protocols because they are not rituals in the usual sense. They are ways of being, ways of seeing, thinking, and feeling. We refer to them as Protocols because they have nothing to do with candles, summoning spirits, or other styles of magickal work.

The Protocols enable you to encourage a stronger connection with your Angel. You become open to the Angel and focus on the required work to make yourself perceptive, so that the connection can be achieved easily.

What you discover here might not feel like magick, most of the time, but you will find it takes you on journeys and reveals its depth and complexity as you progress. During some stages, the experience will be undeniably magickal, and your sense of the Angel will grow ever more tangible.

You can read ahead if you like, to see what the Protocols entail, but as mentioned above, they will not sound like spectacular magick. They are often about spending a short time thinking, remembering, or observing. It can appear all too ordinary, but as has been suggested many times in this text, what seems simple is often the most profound.

You are free to use the Protocols in any way that you like, and I have learned in recent years that overly prescriptive advice is rarely followed by eager readers. If I tell you exactly what to do, it won't work so well. If I leave you to go on an adventure and find out what's best for you, it will work beautifully.

I understand, however, that it is easier to work with *some* guidance. Indeed, some readers would prefer a set schedule where you're told the exact length and timing of each Protocol.

So, I'll give you some guidance on how to get into this and a structure that you can follow, but then you should allow yourself to make up your mind and be guided by experience.

You may wonder why I don't set out a rigid timetable, and there is a good reason. If I said you should use the first Protocol for a week, and then perform the second Protocol for a week, and so on, you'd get a very firm expectation that in seven weeks, something would happen. That's the exact opposite of what I believe is going to help you. Approaching a deadline like that is counter-productive, and setting a timeline can be misleading. Some things will take days, some will take months, and because the benefits begin straight away, there is no need to rush through. Even when the Protocols are complete, you may continue with them or repeat them all.

I believe you should go into this knowing something can happen on day one, while also knowing that it will take as long as it takes. There is no predicting what will happen when because everybody starts from a different place, and everybody has a different journey.

What I usually advise is that you should work with great intention but without anxious need. I understand that this may be the most difficult part of the work. Why should you keep going if there aren't quick and easy results? For many people, there will be indications of the Angel's reality from very early on, while others will need much more patience. But I also think that for almost everybody, there will be periods where it feels pointless, and only your determination to continue will take you through. I cannot give you that determination. That is what you must bring to the process. And although I use the word determination, that does not mean desperation. I like to compare this to eager novelists who write for the love of it, without any guarantee their work will be published. They work *as though* the work will be published, diligently writing every day and assuming everything will be ok and that readers will one day enjoy their work. They hope for publication, but they don't worry. They believe that publication is inevitable and so they get on with the writing. That is what you must do with your magick.

Whatever else you decide, use Protocol One first, as this is the primary Protocol that shapes the rest of the experience. I usually advise sticking with Protocol One every day in some form or another, even if it's in a small way. To be clear, you could use nothing but Protocol One and you could achieve everything you want from this book. So even when you introduce additional Protocols, I suggest that you also find time for Protocol One every day.

After some time (and it might be days or weeks), you then introduce the second Protocol. After a while longer, you can work with the third Protocol. If you wish, and if you can find the time, you can continue with all these Protocols at the same time. That is, of course, quite time-consuming, so an alternative approach is to cease working with earlier Protocols as you add in new ones. Most people will find that working with a few Protocols at once is fine. You don't need to force more magick into your life than feels comfortable.

You may be wondering how you are meant to know when to move on from the first Protocol. Should you wait a week, or a month, or until there's a sign, omen, or some indication that things are happening? The best way to get started is to forget about these details. There is no need to decide what you will do in advance, so long as you commit to *beginning* the magick and *continuing* with the magick. No harm comes if you stop, of course, but the solid intention to work with this magick in a deep way is more effective than testing it out to see what you think of it all.

Once you are underway, you will often get a strong urge to introduce another Protocol, and when you do, that is the right time. It might be after a week, or it might take months. If you never get that urge, you are free to introduce a Protocol whenever you feel like it, when you have the time. No harm will come from this. I believe, however, that most people will benefit from steady progress. The aim is not to get them done or put them out of the way, but to get so used to them that they change the way you perceive the world. Be prepared for this to take time, and remember that you are not seeking a golden moment of revelation, but something that brings benefits and power for the rest of your life.

Also, when starting out, it really helps to know that when you get to the Seventh Protocol, there's no participation award. At that point, even if you've made strong contact with the Angel, you will almost certainly continue with some of the Protocols because they are an effective way to maintain the connection. Your Angel will possibly instruct you in other ways to maintain the connection, but that is not something I can elaborate upon as it will be entirely personal to you. But as I said, don't see this as a list of Protocols to be ticked off so you expect your Angel to appear like a prize. Most people will settle into using the Protocols in various combinations.

You can, of course, come back to an earlier Protocol at any time you want. You will learn to trust your intuition regarding what magick you require. Try to get used to the unstructured nature of this method. But be willing to spend weeks, or more, with a Protocol, if that feels right.

There is no timetable to follow and no rules that can be broken. When you begin to work with the Protocols, and when you begin to sense your Angel, a timeline, plan, or schedule imposed by me, or any other, would be irrelevant. Put aside expectations or timelines and know that attaining the Angel is more important than achieving the connection on a particular day on your calendar.

Be willing to enjoy whatever benefits occur in the early stages. Enjoy the progress you make, even if the level of contact you seek doesn't come as fast as you want. The more you enjoy and appreciate the benefits, the stronger the connection becomes.

Although I have spoken of commitment, there is no danger in taking time off if you become unwell for any reason, or if you feel that you would prefer to concentrate on other magick or other aspects of your life. Momentum is beneficial, though, and the more committed you are, the more likely you are to progress. Commitment means that, even when nothing appears to be happening and progress has apparently halted or reversed, you keep going.

You don't need to let the magick take over your life, but you may find that having the magick continue daily, can help you through any of the challenges in your life. This magick gives you the chance to focus on a higher purpose which can remove the sting of everyday problems.

It is possible to take commitment too far and attempt too much at once. If you think you'll get better results by doing all seven Protocols at once, every day, you *may* be correct, but you could easily be wrong. Often, people do lots and lots of magick in the hope that it will force things to happen. But that denies the subtle nature of this work. Also, you don't want to burn out, or feel overwhelmed, or rush through this so fast that you don't settle into each Protocol. Your experience is important and if you try to do too much at once, your experience will be shallower.

Often, the most beneficial work does not become evident until long after it was performed, and so you will not be able to make an accurate judgment about the objective value of a Protocol. You will, however, gain an intuition about what feels right, what you enjoy doing, or what you sense is needed, and this intuition will serve you well. If you don't feel any intuition about this, that is fine, and you can choose to work through the Protocols in any systematic way you choose. Begin with the first Protocol, assume that your Angel is already guiding you, and then continue with the other Protocols in any way that works for you, and see what happens.

As you work through the Protocols you should begin to sense the Angel in some way. That is, of course, the purpose of the book. It could be the recognition of more synchronicity in your life. It could be a feeling of presence, or a gentle sense of guidance and protection. It may be a general sensation of being helped. There could be moments that feel almost holy, as though you see beyond the ordinary. And for some people, there could be a connection that is much more obvious and undeniable.

What happens if you sense absolutely nothing? If you spend several weeks working with the Protocols as suggested, and nothing at all happens even after all that effort, what then? I believe something *will* happen, and the more you sense these changes and moments of connection, the more likely they are to happen. You may have fear, reservation, doubt, resistance, and many other problems that appear to keep the Angel at a distance, but this is all an illusion. If you do the work, and become open to sensing the Angel (which is what the Protocols help you to achieve), I do not think it is possible to sense absolutely nothing.

If you think nothing has happened, it can only mean that you have yet to become open to sensing the results. If that happens, don't feel that it's all over and that you have failed. Try again when you feel ready, and be as relaxed as you can. If you think you rushed, slow down. If you think you were too desperate, be more at ease. If you feel you're doing something wrong, you are probably overthinking the process. If you think you don't have the ability, you are blissfully wrong.

From everything I have seen, for more than half my life working with this magick, I do not believe there will be a problem. If you do the work, you will sense something, and you will notice beneficial changes in your life. Acknowledge the first glimpses of contact and you will attract more. It may be subtle, or it may be dramatic. Whatever you get, trust it, be grateful for it, and the connection will grow.

You may find that the Protocols have such power that you wish to stay within some of them for a long time. Some people use them as a stepping stone to contact, and others stay with them forever, letting them remain a way of being open to magickal possibility. This is a choice you will make and your wisdom will be informed by your Angel. Learning to navigate through the magickal contact is part of the magickal process itself. You may even choose to stop working with the Protocols. Your Angel will not leave you. As such, you may stop working with the Protocols, and you will still benefit from the work you have done. Some people choose to continue, but use the Protocols less frequently, strengthening the connection very gradually. Others want to know the potential of Complete Contact and that is explored later in the book, when you get to The Quest for Contact.

You may change your mind about what you want, and how much you want, as you work with the methods. This is not a race and you are not trying to attain any sort of proof. Allow yourself to change and adapt as the magick becomes a part of your life. Your Angel will reward your efforts to make contact.

I expect that you will discover a sense of bliss, safety, and excitement. You will continue to live your life, faced with problems and difficulties, but you may find that you feel protected, wise, and blessed. Even when everything falls apart, as it will do while the cycles of your life continue to turn, you will feel supported. Should you choose to proceed no further, that will be acceptable.

You can use this book at the same time as any other magick that's in your life. Some readers will find this works well and others will prefer to focus on this magick alone, at least for a while.

It is important to me that any book I write should be self-contained. You do not need to seek out other books in order to make this one effective. Everything you need is contained in this book, even if you are a beginner. It is also true that I have, in the past, suggested that my book *Mystical Words of Power* is a good preparation for connecting with your Angel. That is certainly true, and indeed the methods found there are a way of opening up to the powers described here, and to some extent, that book covers similar ground. Its purpose is not to connect with the Angel directly, but the methods bring your Angel into your sphere of influence indirectly. If you have worked with that book, you may find it easier to begin working with this one. If you have not worked with that book, please do not think you have to do so. It is self-contained and optional. You can begin working with *this* book right now, even if you've never read about any other magick before. If you want to use *Mystical Words of Power* at the same time as this one, that is also fine, but please remember that you don't *need* to. Everything you need is here.

Protocol One: Intentional Opening

Protocol One is a direct act of intention, reaching out to sense the Angel, physically, emotionally, mentally. In many ways, this is the most obvious method, and one you may already have tried. If you have never tried it, or if you have tried it a hundred times, please work with this consistently and observe what happens.

Find some time to be alone without disturbance. There is no need to sit, kneel, stand, lie down, or be in any particular position, but remain comfortable. Slouching doesn't create the best mental atmosphere, but you aren't required to sit in any difficult position or to be motionless. All you need to do is feel that you are settled in a way that is appropriate for this kind of magick. There is no need to light candles or incense. You can, but I wouldn't because being able to do this often is more important than adding any ceremony.

Whether you are sitting or standing, open your arms so that your palms are facing upward. This is similar to the gesture you would make to an old friend, meaning they should come in for a hug. This gesture is an act of welcoming and despite its simplicity, is an extremely powerful way to invite the Angel. Of course, just opening your arms with your palms facing up does nothing in itself, but you are doing this with the *intention* of welcoming your Angel. That makes all the difference.

Do not be afraid that this gesture will invite all manner of evil spirits. I know from the messages I've received that people are afraid of summoning the wrong entity, or attracting an evil spirit at the wrong moment. Remember, your intention here is to contact the Angel. The moment you decide to make this attempt, your Angel knows what you are doing, and all the protection you require is firmly in place. Your Angel cannot be in the dark about your intention, and therefore it will protect you. By making this gesture with the intention of connecting with your Angel, nothing unwanted will occur.

If you can keep your arms in that position, with the palms turned upwards, do so, but if it's at all uncomfortable, then let your arms relax. You have made the gesture and that will be enough. (I would sometimes cross my arms over my chest, or just relax them. I learned early on that the initial moment of making this gesture is far more important than trying to hold the position.)

Now you mentally intend to sense your Angel. This is nothing more than reaching out to sense the presence of the Angel. As I said earlier, most people have never tried to contact the Angel, so this is the moment in which you do.

You may find this so easy that it requires no instruction. You may find that you can mentally reach for the Angel and attempt to sense its reality. You know it is an intelligent spirit, closer to you than anybody or anything else could be in this world, and you reach out to make contact. If you can do that, go ahead. If not, and if you have no idea what to do, you may prefer to use words. Some people run words through their mind. You may think something like, 'Are you there, are you with me?' Or you could modify this to be something more like, 'I know you are there. I intend to know you.' You could also phrase this as a question, such as, 'I intend to know you, will you know me?' As you think these things, always know that the Angel *is* present and *can* hear you.

These examples are brief, simple, and by no means the whole story because part of the magickal process is that you discover what works for you by making the attempt to reach out to the Angel in *whatever* way occurs to you. I have mentioned already that this book is deliberately brief, given how massive the subject matter is, and I cannot stress this enough; brevity is more important than too much detail because your own discoveries are as important as anything I offer. If you find yourself longing for more direct instruction, please know the importance of seeking your own answers.

If you have absolutely no idea what to do, then first make the gesture with your palms, intend to know your Angel (even if you're not sure what that means), and then simply observe what you feel in the following minutes as you think about the Angel and what it might be to you. You intend to connect with your Angel, and you intend to sense its reality in some way, even if you don't know what that will be yet. Do this every day, and you will discover methods that work for you.

At this point I wouldn't blame you for wondering how this can work. All I've said is that you open your arms with your palms up and try to sense the Angel. That might sound like the most disappointing, obvious, and unmagickal act you could perform. I understand that when you want to discover new magick there is the desire to find something special, mystical, or obviously exciting about the method. What you've just read will sound so dull, you might wonder why we're excited by this book. My answer is that we only ever look for magick that works, and although the method is simple - almost too simple to feel worthwhile - it can work with great intensity.

I would never dress workable magick up in exciting ceremony to make it seem more impressive. I know there are some people who are eager for exciting words of power or elaborate sigils that can reveal the Angel, and others who hope I'll update the traditional methods into something flashier. I hope it's clear that I will not go down that path just to make the book more exciting. Later in the book, there *are* sigils and energy-raising methods that might seem more exciting, but please don't underestimate the work revealed in this chapter, or those that follow. Powerful magick often remains secret because it seems too simple, too basic and untheatrical to be effective.

My suggestion is that you suspend disbelief and see what happens. You are already involved with the workings of this book, and the magick will come through to you. Of course, nothing may happen for some time, so intentionally reaching out for the Angel requires some commitment, and you may find it difficult to motivate yourself. What I hope will motivate you is expecting and believing that this *might* work. Unlike the traditional methods, which involved intense prayer over countless, isolated months, you are only spending a few moments or minutes reaching out for the Angel each day.

You will begin to sense that seeing beyond the obvious is a very important part of this process. If you insist that this is a pointless exercise, it will be, but if you accept that it is an intentional act of real magick, it becomes the most vital step to making a closer connection to your Angel. Your Angel is with you, and there may have been many times, whether they were moments of inspiration, unexpected joy, luck, protection, or something else altogether more personal, where you will have felt the Angel's support and presence, even if you had no idea that connection was there. Now, you are making the connection intentional and allowing it to become more tangible. And this, simple as it sounds, will be the main way you open yourself to a connection unlike any other in your life.

There may be a sound, a voice, a change in temperature, or just the briefest shiver that makes you know something is happening. When you perform this Protocol, it is an act of intention, but the final part of the process should always be that you become quiet and receptive, noticing whatever you can.

I cannot give overly specific instructions on how long you should spend in this state. I can say that you don't need to sit there for an hour, reaching for the Angel. For most people, a few moments or minutes will be sufficient. You will know when you have enacted your intention. You will know when you have opened to the Angel, and given some time to sense its reality. You cannot set a timer on this work. Sometimes you will decide to end the Protocol after a few seconds, and other times you may bask in it for quite a while. When you are done, there is no closing ceremony. You simply go back to ordinary life. You continue with the Protocol every day for as long as feels right. If you miss a day or a week, nothing bad can happen, but there is rarely a reason to miss a day.

As you work with this Protocol, please remember that there is no rush, and as soon as you begin to reach for the Angel, the Angel is reaching for you. Always recall the instructions from the chapter *Receiving The Angel*. They remain an essential part of the work for the rest of the book.

Protocol Two: The Angel's Support

Throughout this book, I have stressed that this magick is not about problem-solving and managing the details of everyday life. And yet, the Angel *will* become involved in many of your future decisions, and will help you find the best pathway through any situation where you sincerely need help. So, yes, it will help you solve problems when they really matter. And this is the crux of the matter. Sincere need.

At this stage, you will connect strongly with the Angel when your need is real, when you feel unable to solve a problem without assistance. If you don't need help, then don't ask the Angel. If you're struggling to decide which shoes to wear, you should handle that on your own.

Your Angel is there for you when you need help, when you feel you cannot solve a problem by yourself, and so, although I have said that the purpose of this book is not to reveal problem-solving magick, you can, in fact, work with the Angel to solve problems. I did not want to announce this with great fanfare because it is not the purpose of the book or the magickal work that you do here. But it is part of the process of engaging with your Angel. Indeed, seeking the Angel's help in times of sincere need is one of the ways to form a closer bond. The second Protocol is all about recognising those moments of need, and asking the Angel for help.

In magick, when we seek help from a spirit, there is usually a ritual involving some form of chant, a sequence of emotional and mental actions, and perhaps the use of a sigil or other physical form that represents a connection to that spirit.

We call on divine forces and other powers to bring that Angel into our presence to hear our commands or requests. With your own Guardian Angel, there is no such ceremony. What you are aiming for is a state where you know that the Angel is always with you, and so any sincere request for help, made silently in your own mind, will be heard by your Angel.

The key is to know that you are not talking to yourself when you ask for help. You must know that you are making the request *to* your Angel. Do that, and you will always be heard, and there will always be some form of response, whether you notice it or not.

I could almost end this chapter here, keeping it as brief as that because this is just about the only instruction you need. But having worked with many people during this phase, I know that it raises doubts and questions. This is when people begin to worry about how to talk to the Angel, whether or not they are doing things correctly, and whether their requests are genuine.

The first thing to establish is that you do not need to worry too much about getting it right. Magick is an opportunity, offered to those who discover it, and it is not a force that attempts to block you. This is not an obstacle course, but a clear and open path. In terms of this magick, your Angel does not sit on high, waiting for you to get it right. You are not being judged. Your magickal attempts are not being analysed. The Angel is never waiting for you to do magick properly. All that's happening is that your always-present Angel is forming a close bond with you, at your behest. Keep that in mind as you work with this Protocol.

If you want to get good at playing the piano, there's nothing quite like playing the piano. You should play often, sometimes in a relaxed manner, sometimes with more discipline. Lessons can help. Buying a great piano can help a little, but you can do well with a more basic model. Studying theory can be of great benefit if you know how to apply it to your technique. But nothing is as important as playing the piano with enjoyment. If you want to get into improvisation, instruction is less important than letting go of your inhibitions and allowing the music to emerge as you play. It takes a lot of practice to become skilled enough to reach the point where you can improvise, but when you reach that point, letting go of the need to be right is almost the point. To become a great improviser, you must be willing to fail. If you reach for beautiful music while knowing that you may fail, your improvisation can be utterly stunning. When you work with this magick, you are letting go of many structures and rules, and learning to improvise the magick that comes from within you. I cannot say that this is easy, but it should be easier than improvising Jazz piano. You don't need to become an expert at magick. You are already an expert in asking for help, at feeling the need for help, and that is all you need, if you are willing to let go of trying to create perfect magick.

I will share another example offered by a colleague that I think helps to show a good approach to this Protocol. You learn to ride a bicycle by getting on and trying to ride. You know you might fall off, and you try not to fall, learning from every wobble. Balance comes from being unbalanced at first. This is a stage where you should keep all these instructions in mind, but feel free to be unbalanced. If you feel like a beginner who's making mistakes, that's to be expected and is often an essential part of your progress.

Even so, you may worry that your needs are not sincere enough, and that you shouldn't bother your Angel with them. I know this is a common problem for people at this stage, but you should know that although I have urged you to focus on sincere needs, you don't need to be concerned about getting this right. It might be worth remembering that you are not looking for worthy needs. There is no need to impress the Angel or suggest that your need is in some way spiritual. Your need might be quite materialistic. All that matters is that you care about it deeply. If your desire is to buy something new and expensive, it may be a truly sincere need. Or it may be nothing more than retail therapy. Knowing the difference is all that matters.

I spend a reasonable amount of time working with young artists these days, and occasionally there is an overlap with magick. But sometimes, magick doesn't need to be involved for me to see the difference between true need and distracting desire. I worked with two students who were studying in the same class, and one became hyper-focussed on purchasing new equipment. This equipment included a camera for collecting reference images, a new laptop for storing images, and a wealth of art materials that were all of a high quality. It was a huge expense, even though she came from a wealthy family, and I felt that she was merely creating a barrier to her own work. Although good tools are effective, it's better to work freely with any tools, even tools that you make, than it is to wait for the right time to create your art. The same is true with magick, and it's better to work imperfectly than to keep waiting. But there was another student, and she too had a strong desire for certain expensive equipment that would help her work on a substantial new project. In her case, the need was real. Her need did not stop her from working, but her desire for the new equipment was real because it meant she would be able to expand her creative work. As this played out before me, it was a textbook demonstration of the difference between distracting desires and true needs.

You may worry that asking the Angel for something that isn't a true need could be dangerous or counter-productive, but you are safe. If you get it wrong, the worst that can happen is nothing at all. Or, you may get what you thought you wanted, only to find that it's a hollow victory. I can remember several occasions when I was quite young, where I used a whole range of magick to achieve goals that were poorly planned. They were based on what I thought might make me happy. But those weren't real needs. They were pretty basic desires for things that didn't affect me in a positive way. After five minutes, that shiny new object is often a purchase you regret. But was that wasted time or wasted magick? Not at all. It was brilliant learning. So, you cannot go wrong.

Although I have urged you to work with this magick only when your need is sincere, you won't be punished or shunned by your Angel if you aren't certain about your real needs. You can be relaxed about working with this Protocol, but also know it is here for a reason. Working through your thoughts and feelings, learning about the difference between what you think you want and what you really need, is more important to this process than you can imagine. It is a significant act of practical magick. You don't have to get it right or solve all your problems, but making a connection with the Angel becomes easier when you hand over your real needs to your Angel.

The beauty of this Protocol is that it's not something you have to plan for. You work with the magick as the need arises. You will probably find it beneficial to keep working with Protocol One at the same time. What if you've reached this part of the book and have no sincere needs? I have yet to meet somebody who is utterly content, so I find that unlikely. If there is nothing that you want to work on, you can leave this Protocol until you do have something in mind. Others may find they wish to work with this every day, for some time, with need after need occurring.

Sincere needs come in many flavours. Your need for a new television could be sincere if watching films is something you value. For some people, a new television might be nothing more than a time-filling distraction, but to you, it could be something you need to enjoy your hobby of film-watching. Don't assume that your need is superficial just because it's often judged that way by others. What matters to you, matters. Also, enjoy those moments when you realise you are quite content with what you have, right now, enjoying the privilege of your existence. These moments might be rarer, but no matter what your circumstances, they can occur. Learning to appreciate what I had, even when I was at my most desolate, lost, lonely, and impoverished, was the way I began to rise.

You may have a few quite specific needs, to solve an immediate and obvious problem. Or you may want to change something more fundamental about yourself or your life. You may know, for example, that your attitude to money is not great, and that your feelings could be hampering your effort to create wealth. When you hate money, money stays away. So your need could be to work on that foundation within yourself, so you can feel at peace with wealth, without falling for the trappings of greed. And there are other obvious needs that don't need much explanation. If you feel anxious or lonely, those are fundamental aspects of your life that you want to change, even if there's no immediate solution that you can imagine. The problems you try to solve with magick may be quite specific and immediate, or they may be more general. If it feels like a need to you, then it is something you can work with here.

If there's a problem you could solve with simpler magick, use that for now. And if you could solve a problem without any magick, try that. You may find that the Angel begins to bring unexpected help when tackling these other needs, but don't expect it at this stage. For the Angel's help, look to problems that seem impossible to solve in any other way.

A problem that some people face is that they have so many needs, they don't know where to start. Take your time, slowly and gently, to share your problems with your Angel. Remember, the purpose of this Protocol isn't actually to get magickal results. You are asking for help because the act of asking is a way to reach your Angel. This is how you increase your conscious connection to the Angel. And that means you shouldn't see this as the way to solve all your problems. The trick to getting this right is that - even though you are sincerely asking for help - you shouldn't even expect results. This may seem like a bizarre contradiction, but as I said earlier, you are not asking for help with trivial matters.

When working with magick, we often say that you should avoid desperation. It is true that magick works best when you lose the feeling of urgency. Many of the rituals we have published have systems built into them that help you with this process. But there are still some areas where you may feel a sense of hopelessness or desperation. For this Protocol, it is quite acceptable to feel desperate. And, in truth, if a need is really deep and sincere, it may feel so important that you find it impossible to let go of your desire. And yet, you will. In handing your problem to the Angel and letting it deal with the problem for you, you may immediately feel some sense of ease.

Earlier in the book, I talked about manifesting at will, and that will be covered more as you progress. It may even happen when you work with this Protocol, but it is absolutely essential to remember that this is not your goal. If you spend months asking for results from your Angel, and nothing seems to happen, not a moment has been wasted because every time you ask, the Angel comes nearer to you. And remember, the instructions are as simple as knowing the Angel is real and can hear you, and asking for help in whatever way feels right. You never need to convince the Angel that your need is sincere or worthy; you don't need to fawn or beg. You only state what is wrong, what you want to change, and ask for help with sincerity. It usually takes only moments.

One of my favourite analogies, used by many occultists, is to think about how it feels when you talk to somebody in the next room. I'm not referring to those moments when everybody's shouting at each other, hoping to be heard, and yet everybody's struggling to hear. I'm talking about those times when you know somebody you care about is within earshot, but in the next room. You know that although you cannot see them, they will hear you. They are not present, but their presence is felt. You speak to an empty room, but you will be heard. This feeling is the same when you speak to the Angel. It is not visible, it is not obviously present, it feels like you are talking to yourself in an empty room, but you know you can be heard. If it helps, remember this each time you ask for help. Keep it brief, keep it simple, and then move on. As always, there is no closing ceremony, and nothing else to do. You have asked, so you can return to your ordinary life, and perhaps, in the following days, it will become a little less ordinary.

Protocol Three: Active Intention

This Protocol involves performing physical actions with the intention that they will help you make contact with your Angel. Some of the ways you can do this are quite obvious, but others will require more explanation.

Throughout the history of magick, gestures have been used as a form of ritual. Even the first Protocol in this book uses the gesture of the open arms with your palm facing upward. The idea is that by performing a repeated motion, that has meaning and intention, it becomes far more than a simple act of movement. It becomes magick as soon as you want it to be magick.

The third Protocol is easily described, and this chapter will be brief, but I found this to be one of the best methods for improving my connection to the Angel.

If I say that you should go for a walk, you will go for a walk, and there is nothing magickal about that. But if I tell you to go for a walk as a magickal act, with every step taking you closer to your Angel, that is a powerful ritual. Ordinary actions become magickal.

It doesn't have to be a walk, and I have even suggested that almost any physical activity will work, especially when you repeat the same action. I have encountered cynicism when running this idea past students, and when sharing an early copy of this book. One person said, 'So I'm meant to crochet my way to the Angel?' I could see her point. It sounds mundane and silly when put like that. My answer was that while climbing mountains might seem more mystical and grander, any act that brings you joy can work. That might even be crochet. But it should be something you enjoy, without it feeling like an obligation.

I was also asked if sex could be used, but that's a complicated one because you either become too involved with the sex, or too involved with the act of reaching for the Angel. It's not impossible, but it's not what I'd recommend.

I suggest that you find something simple and enjoyable that can easily fit into your daily routine. It might be as ordinary as cooking a meal, going for a walk, or taking a shower. The point is that during this time, you perform the act as though you believe the physical actions are magickal actions. You don't actually have to believe this at first, although you should come to believe it over time.

I also recommend sticking to the same action. For me, it was always walking. Mostly, I wouldn't be interrupted, and I could look around, enjoying the world, always keeping in mind what this walk was for. And that is the only difficulty; keeping your mind on what you're doing. If you go for a forty-five-minute walk, your mind will wander. So, I suggest starting small, and building this up. Or, you can use this Protocol quite briefly. I know some people have created physical gestures, using their bodies or arms (in something akin to yoga or Tai-Chi) that they perform for five minutes a day. That works. So does washing the dishes by hand, if you remember you are not washing the dishes but performing an action with the intention of reaching your Angel.

I understand that this can be hard to grasp, and the cynical response I mentioned is very common. My own response to being given this instruction was that it seemed stupid. I was actually a little angry, at first, because I wanted something very far from ordinary. Back then, I would rather chant mystical words in an eerie room. But I was reminded that we are bringing the Angel into our ordinary world. That is the purpose of this work, and so the ordinary should be a part of that. You take an ordinary task and tweak it with intention.

It is amusing, when looked at from an outside perspective, that many eager occultists are happy to wear robes, burn herbs, chant strange words, and conjure up spirits of all kinds, but when you ask them to do something quite ordinary, they get upset. I do empathise, and if this seems too much for you to swallow, just move on for now. But one day, I trust you'll find value in this idea.

If any of these Protocols don't appeal, leave them alone for now. The Angel won't ignore you because you skipped a Protocol. If you don't find one of them helpful, move on. But be willing to revisit an unwanted Protocol at a later time. You will change during this process, so be willing to see how your interaction with magick changes. What once seemed irrelevant could become useful at a later date.

Although I have suggested picking one action, such as going for a walk, it doesn't have to be something new. If you go to the gym every day, you could use that. All you have to do is change the way you go to the gym; you go with far less focus on your fitness, and far more focus on using each movement to become closer to the Angel. Use something that's already in your life. As I say though, at first, you may only be able to keep the intention clear for a few minutes or moments. In time, working with intention for an hour or more becomes quite easy, although you are not required to push this. If the joy goes out of it, then it becomes pointless.

Some people use this Protocol just once a month or less. Others prefer to use it every day. Most like to use the same physical action each time, as I suggest, but some prefer to think of a new action each time they perform the ritual. Personally, I find that too demanding and distracting, but if it works for you, that's fine. All that matters is that you remember, each time, that you are doing this for a reason. You are doing this - whatever it may be - for the purpose of being close to your Angel. If you are walking, you are not just walking around the block, you are walking to strengthen your connection to the Angel. If you are eating something delicious, you are not just enjoying that food, but eating and enjoying as an act of internal connection.

What happens if you're interrupted or distracted, or if somebody speaks to you while you're in the middle of this? Nothing. Bring your attention back to your intention. It doesn't have to be regimented and it shouldn't be difficult. When I went for my first intentional walks, I thought I had to take every step with great willpower and yearning. That's unsustainable and absolutely not required. You can even let your mind wander. Just make sure that, whatever your physical action, every now and then, you recall why you are doing this.

You can even work with this Protocol without taking any direct physical action. You could, for example, make the act of travelling from one place to another be your intentional activity. I know that people take something ordinarily dull, such as sitting on a subway train, and use it as their process. This works well, because even though you aren't actually doing anything obvious, things are changing. You move from one place to another and enormous change occurs. Feel free to try this more passive approach, but also be aware it may not be right for you. For most people, something simple and physical works perfectly.

The only warning that comes with this is a mundane one, where I strongly recommend you retain your perception of the outside world. It's not safe to walk in most places without an awareness of the landscape, people, and traffic. If you are driving, you must focus on driving. Even if you're sitting on a train, you need to be aware of your surroundings. Never use this Protocol in a way that distracts you when such distraction could be dangerous. You are not performing this Protocol to block out or forget the world. Whatever you do, whether active or passive, you are only holding the thought that you are performing the intention to connect with your Angel. It does not require tremendous focus. I think of it as being similar to driving over to a friend's house. Some of the time, you might think about your friend, you might even imagine what you'll talk about, but most of the time you'll think about other things and focus on driving; but the whole time, you know where you're going. You know you're driving to your friend's house.

Use the Protocol in this way, and you stay safe in the ordinary world, while still enacting the Protocol. As has been said many times, it is the intention that matters,

I will add one further suggestion, and that is to perform a physical action that has no purpose. Instead of turning an ordinary activity into something magickal, you perform a new activity as an act of magick. This could be a repeated movement of your arms, a dance, clapping, walking around in a circle, or anything else that appeals. For some people, especially those seeking privacy, this can be ideal, although the unusual nature of this action can make you feel ridiculous. This is often a challenge with magick, especially when you start out. Many readers have told me that the first few times they performed a ritual they felt utterly ridiculous, and even ashamed for believing this might work. Only when it worked did that feeling go away. It isn't like that for everybody, and some people are able to perform actions without inhibition or embarrassment. But if walking around your room in circles makes you feel ridiculous, find something else.

If the instructions seem too brief, and you're still wondering what you could possibly do, try not to overthink the process, and don't be in a rush. Give this some thought for a few days and it may become obvious. Whatever you choose doesn't have to stay the same, either. For one week you might use playing the piano as your intentional action, and the next week you may decide to turn your lunches into a few minutes of sacred intention. If you have no ideas at all, simply do what I always did, and take a regular walk.

Whatever you choose, it helps if you can be alone and uninterrupted. Don't choose to use your mealtime for this Protocol if you always eat with colleagues or family. If you eat one meal a day in solitude, however, then eating and enjoying food is one of the best ways to perform this Protocol. You don't need silence or a time completely free of people. On my walks, I would always say hello to the people I passed, and take time to be friendly to the local dogs and cats. You're not in a trance.

All you're doing is making one activity into something more magickal through a decision to let it be magickal.

You can continue to work with the Protocols that have come before. I find that most people get to this stage and find that working with the first three Protocols, every day, is quite manageable.

Although this is one of the least popular Protocols amongst students when they begin, it becomes one of the most beloved, because moments of feedback are quite common. When performing this intentional action, you are more likely to sense, hear, or know the Angel. Don't expect or demand it, but know that it's possible.

I will also add that with these three Protocols, you can achieve great things. There are many people who have achieved all they wanted with these three Protocols alone. You might consider them to be the core rituals, and the foundation for the work that you do here. With nothing else, you can achieve contact, and know the benefits of the Angel. That does not mean that what remains is superfluous. Everything that follows introduces ideas that were gathered and refined to make the process richer, giving you more options for the way you move through this adventure in magick.

Protocol Four: Releasing Pain

The Fourth Protocol is about offering up your pain to the Angel. This is not an offering in the usual magickal sense, where you give a spirit something as payment. You are not paying your Guardian Angel at all, but giving it your pain to ease the burden of pain that you feel. This can be physical pain, emotional pain, or even emotions such as anger, memories of the past damage inflicted on you by others and by circumstance.

Once again, I should remind you that although you act as though the Angel will ease your pain in some way, your purpose is not to seek relief, but to seek connection with the Angel. Your pain, in whatever form it occurs, may be eased, but even if nothing happens, the work is being done and you are drawing the Angel closer.

The Angel already knows you, and what you have been through, so this Protocol is not about sharing knowledge. In recognising moments of pain or damage, and releasing them to the Angel, you are again finding a way to ask the Angel for help. By now, you should be seeing a pattern with some of these Protocols. You seek a benefit, but you don't need or expect the results, even though you know it may occur. Always, you know that these actions help to reveal the Angel and strengthen the connection between you.

The process can be planned out, almost as a ritual, where you gather memories or feelings, and offer them to the Angel. Or it can happen in the moment, where you feel pain, and silently offer the pain to the Angel, asking it to bring you some relief.

I know that when it gets to this point, some people become frustrated. A question I am often asked is, 'How am I meant to offer something to the Angel when I haven't seen or heard it? I don't know it exists, so what do I actually do?' For many readers, by this stage, there will be some tangible sense of the Angel. For others, there will be none, and it can be difficult to know where your feelings are meant to go.

I will say that frustration is to be expected at times, but the cure for this feeling is to try something and see what happens. If you are in pain, notice your pain, and when you are fully aware of that pain, feeling it deeply rather than avoiding it, you can say to the Angel, silently in your mind, 'Take this from me.' You may not need to use words. You may simply choose to offer the pain to the Angel with an act of will, or a moment of decision. You can choose to give the pain away, or you can ask the Angel to take it, or you can do both. As with all the methods in this book, the guidelines are not overly strict and you will discover what you need by experimenting.

Some people feel such strong relief from this method that they systematically work through all their pains, all their emotional stains and scars, and find enormous change occurring. Others may only feel stirrings of ease, and a few will feel nothing at all, at least at this point. Whatever you feel, know that the act of working the ritual is more important than perceived results because each time you do this, the Angel comes closer. Remember again the details given on Receiving the Angel and ensure that those aspects of the work are kept in your life.

If your life is utterly devoid of pain and you have no bad memories, you can move on, but it is rare. You may be cautious about stirring up old memories and buried pain, and I respect that caution. But when you feel able, know that the process is simple. For grief, you only need to recall your loss and you will feel enough of that grief for it to work. If you feel lonely, you only need to catch a hint of how you feel to offer that to the Angel. If you feel damaged by an entire decade of mistakes, made by yourself and others, you can pick it apart and tackle each painful memory over time, or you can offer your overall feeling.

If you find this process stirs things up for you, it's not something you need to work with daily, but I will say that relief and ease are far more common. Many people find that working with all the previous rituals, alongside this one, can be extremely beneficial.

As mentioned earlier, you can plan ahead and sit quietly, bringing memories of pain into your mind, before releasing them to the Angel. No ritual is required, but you might find it helps to perform Protocol One first. Or, at any moment when you are feeling pain, you can offer that to the Angel, and in a second or two, you have performed important magick.

If you find that working with four Protocols is too much, you can drop any of the others. Your progress can be gradual, and how long you spend working with the Fourth Protocol will be your choice. If you find a need for it at a later date, you can, of course, return to it and see what remains to be discovered.

Protocol Five: Perspective

This Protocol requires the use of your imagination, and I know that for some people, this can be challenging. One of the most common complaints I hear about magick is that it requires too much imagery, too much visualisation. I have always tried to remove these visual and imaginary aspects of the magickal process where possible. Sometimes, though, the imagination is required.

Fortunately, imagination is not something that is distant from you. If you have ever felt hunger, that is a physical manifestation of imagination. If you have ever been attracted to another person, longing to be with them, that is an act of emotional imagination. If you've ever wanted the latest shiny object -whether it's a phone, device, car, house – that's your imagination reaching into the future. It doesn't matter how clearly you see any of this; you still have an imagination.

Some people close their eyes, and they cannot imagine what was in front of them a second before. They cannot picture the faces of loved ones, and they cannot imagine their front door. These people are the exception. Most people can imagine those things, and that is enough. If you have that much imagination, you will be fine.

If you have absolutely no visual imagination, you are still going to be ok, because, on some level, you are able to imagine. Your brain can visualise even if you can't see those images; they occur within you. Otherwise, you'd never be able to find your way home, or make your way to the fridge when you're hungry. Imagination, although a powerful magickal tool, is also an absolutely ordinary part of life.

No matter how much I reassure people that their imagination is sufficient for the task at hand, I am aware that it causes a great degree of tension. Many readers will be alarmed by this Protocol and may feel that they don't have the ability to imagine what I describe. I won't waste any more of your time trying to offer reassurance. To see how it works, try doing it as described. If you feel this is too much of a challenge, don't be dissuaded. Give it a go, consistently, and see what happens.

To some extent, what follows requires a degree of playfulness, and a willingness to pretend. I have often said that the only difference between pretending that something is real, and willing something into existence, is the way that you phrase things. We think of pretending as something fake, something that children do to pass the time. We even say something is 'pretend' to mean it's not real. And so, there is resistance to pretending that things are a certain way. That makes what follows a challenge, and I understand that, but please recall that I said this book might be challenging. You should consider accepting this challenge as you'll probably find it is all much easier than you fear.

In reality, I think most readers will find this a breeze, and no challenge at all, but if you find that this feels too playful to be serious magick, know that a willingness to extend your reality through imagination (or through pretending) underlies almost every magickal act.

The aim of this Protocol is to feel at one with your Angel. You achieve this by briefly pretending that you are the Angel, and you see yourself from the Angel's perspective.

When you study the theory of this magick, this approach may not appear to make sense. If your Angel is something that is real, rather than imaginary, why on earth would you pretend to be the Angel. There is an irony to this process, as there often is within magick. By seeing yourself from the Angel's perspective, you make yourself more at one with the Angel. It is a way of meshing your reality with that of the Angel. If this sounds bizarre, I understand, but I can only suggest that you try this to see what can unfold. A few minutes of imaginative exploration can bring you into much closer alignment with your Angel.

When you perform this act of imagination you will see yourself in the third person. That is, it will be like looking at yourself in a photograph or a movie, rather than through your own eyes. You may have experienced this in dreams, or when picturing yourself achieving something. If you have not, you can try it now. Imagine you are the Angel, somewhere slightly above, off to one side, looking down and watching you read this book. Can you imagine what that looks like? If not, make the attempt anyway, and that is sufficient for now.

The Protocol itself involves using your imagination in a slightly more advanced way. The clarity of the images is not as important as what you feel. You should imagine that you actually are the Angel looking down on yourself and feeling great love and compassion. This is how the Angel sees you, and by imagining this, you align yourself with the Angel's reality.

That is all there is to this Protocol. You imagine you are the Angel; you see yourself from its perspective, and you feel love, admiration, compassion, and joy in your existence. You feel as the Angel feels.

What if you struggle to picture things? That is, as I've already explained, fine, and you only need to make the attempt. You may even find it helps to verbalise the situation in your mind. You might say, 'I see you. I love you. I know that you are safe.' It can even help to name yourself. So, I might say to myself, 'You are loved and safe, Damon.' This certainly feels strange, at first, but the act of naming yourself is a powerful way of aligning yourself with the Angel as it separates you from your own reality for just a moment. Even if you are good with imagery, I suggest using this naming process. As you look down at yourself, let the Angel know you and name you.

You can perform this Protocol in the same place, every day, in a planned way, or you can use it at any other moment. If you are outside, sitting in the sunshine, take a moment to imagine you are the Angel, looking down on *you*. The shift in perspective can be quite transformative.

At first, you will probably only be able to do this when all is calm, but as you progress, you may find great benefit in employing this Protocol at more intense emotional moments. If you are in the middle of a discussion, argument, or other challenging situation, take a second to see yourself from the Angel's perspective. Remember to feel love from yourself, as the Angel would feel love.

You don't have to wait for moments of high drama. Seeing yourself from the Angel's perspective, while sitting at the dinner table, in conversation, can be tricky, but also immensely powerful. With practice, you may find you are able to see yourself from an outside perspective even while engaged in deep conversation.

You should not, of course, use this Protocol when driving, crossing the road, or when you are in any place where using your imagination could be a risk to yourself or others.

Don't worry about the details. I have had students ask me repeatedly how high up they should be. Should they picture themselves from a few feet up, or from much higher? Let whatever happens, happen. You will be able to control what you see, but you can also let things develop with ease. Do not become obsessive about getting this right. And whatever you can see will be enough.

You may wonder how long you should perform this Protocol for, and as with so many aspects of this process, I leave that to you. I know that some people achieve a single, brief moment of clarity, and they feel that is enough. Others prefer to practice this Protocol on and off throughout the day. You will find what works most effectively for you.

The beautiful irony of this Protocol is that by pretending, you make something much more real, and I believe that for many people this imaginative work will help bring on the greatest alignment with the Angel.

Working with all of these Protocols at once, every day, may be too demanding, so continue to follow your intuition when it comes to choosing how you work. I recommend, however, that you continue with Protocol One. Using that

Protocol immediately before attempting this one is highly beneficial.

Protocol Six: Recalling

In recent years, mental health professionals have pushed for more mindfulness, with a detached awareness of the moment, where you observe your surroundings and experience without judgment. Based on ancient practices and religious structures, this has proved beneficial to many people. It helps prevent worry and rumination. There is no doubt that, from a magickal perspective, being present in the moment and appreciating whatever you can perceive without labelling or judging it, can be powerfully transformative.

A small problem has arisen. Some people now believe that focussing on the present is all that matters, and that the past is nothing but a meaningless distraction. I am exaggerating slightly, but I have worked with students who have come to believe that you should never reflect on what has gone before. To discard history, or your personal history, is not something that brings progress.

I am not dismissing the value of mindfulness, and as I say above, an ability to be present, to feel joy regardless of your objective circumstances, is an important magickal process. And I fully understand why many people may be urged, quite wisely, to stop overfocussing on the past. All I am pointing out here is that if you feel safe recalling your past, it can help you to know yourself. And that is an important step to knowing your Angel.

In reality, this is largely a non-issue, because most people who practice mindfulness know there is no harm in thinking about the past. Thoughtful reflection is valuable, whereas cycles of rumination, regret, and shame are not helpful. Most people know this, and I think it should be clear what I am getting at. I'm not offering any mental health advice, or commenting on mindfulness itself, but trying to remind you that your past has value. The past has shaped you, and thinking about it can help you find meaning.

For artists, letting the mind wander, allowing yourself to ruminate, to think, to imagine, and to explore your past is vital. By knowing what led you to be who you are now, you are more able to be present, more able to create. A similar process can work with magick. How you came to be who you are is a mysterious process. Random chance, the choices of others, your environment, and millions of conscious and subconscious decisions led you to become who you are. Delving into this is about more than pondering your past, but is a way to look at who you are beneath the circumstances you have lived through.

The life you led until now can be difficult to recall, challenging to deal with, and for some people, too traumatic. If you do not want to explore the way your past led you to where you are, that is fine, and this Protocol may not be of use to you. If it disturbs you at all, or feels like it will dredge up too many difficult emotions, you can leave this Protocol for now. But remain open to the possibility that it may be useful one day. You should also know that when people do this work, they are protected and guided by the Angel, so nothing comes up that is too difficult to deal with. But I will let you decide whether or not this feels useful to you now.

If you feel willing to look at your past, this Protocol is an excellent way to make magickal progress and feel a deeper connection to your Angel. It is not an act of self-exploration for the sake of it. Your intention, as always with these Protocols, is to connect with the Angel.

You don't have to recall the most difficult or disturbing parts of your life. When using the different versions of the Protocol that follow, pick something you can remember easily. It can be from earlier today, a month ago, or something from any time previously. Overall, what you're doing here is looking at how you came to be who you are, and who you really are.

Version One

Before you begin this process, recall that you are doing this to know yourself, with the intention of knowing your Angel. Try to keep this feeling with you throughout.

Then spend some time thinking about a significant moment in your life. Think about what you actively did to change things, and notice how things then progressed. Was there a difference between what you hoped for and what actually happened? Did your actions always make things work out as expected? Did your actions make any difference at all? Were there moments of random chance that seemed like bad luck or great fortune? What about moments of synchronicity that were as life-changing as any of the efforts you put in? You may not know the answers, but all you are doing is making a guess for what the answers might be.

You are not limited to thinking about one moment in each session. You may find that you are drawn to explore many other aspects of your life. You will know, by now, that I don't put any time limits on such work. It may be over in a few minutes, or you may explore for hours. If your intention is to connect with the Angel, and to know the Angel is supporting your exploration efforts, you cannot go wrong.

Version Two

In the second version of the Protocol, you again begin by reminding yourself that this process is an active way of connecting with the Angel. Keep that intention in mind as you work. You can pick a moment from your past (it can be one you've used in the first version, or something new) and then imagine how you might have acted differently. Think about what might have been different. One small change could have been significant, or perhaps it would have taken a whole sequence of changes to make things different. You can even imagine what would have happened if you'd used magick to make changes, or how things would have been if you were able to radically change your personality or skills at will. It may require a little imagination to guess how things could have changed, but you have the ability to use your imagination in this way.

Version Three

In the third version, you again remind yourself of the intention to connect with the Angel. You then observe a past incident as though you are the Angel. This is an adaptation of Protocol Five. You imagine that you are the Angel at a moment in the past, and you watch yourself with compassion and love. Whatever you are doing in the memory, whether you are making mistakes or achieving glories, you look on from above as though you are the Angel, caring, supporting, never judging, and always wanting the best. It can take some time to get used to this process, and seeing yourself without judgment may take practice. Don't worry if you can't get it right at first. Trying to achieve this is enough, and as with all visual aspects, if you only have the vaguest feelings, rather than clear images, you are still doing good, useful imaginative work.

You don't have to use all three versions on any given day. Generally, I think most people have sufficient concentration to work with one or two. If you find yourself using all three, you are free to do that, but never let yourself become exhausted by the process, or you may begin to resent the work.

This Protocol requires more input from you than most of the others, and although you can do it while sitting in a park or riding the train into the city, you may find you benefit from this most when you set aside a peaceful time to allow yourself to explore. Whether you engage for a minute or much longer, the benefits will be real.

You should know that you are not daydreaming about the past, or engaging in wishful thinking. These three versions of the Protocol are magickal processes that connect you to the feeling of change, to the knowledge that choice is often available. They also remind you that sometimes things happen for no obvious reason. They connect you to the sense of flowing chaos we live through, and the moments of decision and control that guide our lives. You are not meant to sit there feeling proud, ashamed or dismayed about your life. You're just reviewing some key moments, and knowing that the Angel has been there, caring for you, whatever you did, and whatever happened.

Protocol Seven: Manifesting at Will

Earlier in the book, I spoke about how the Angel can, in time, help you manifest your desires at will. Without the need for ritual or formal magick, you can choose what you want to happen and see it become so. This does not mean there is no need for other magick because for some people, working with other magick remains an important part of the manifestation process. I continue to use many forms of magick, but as I said, I do not feel the need to be performing rituals every day. Working my will through the power of the Angel is often the easier way.

Now is the time to begin manifesting at will, but please remember that there is a slight twist to this. As with everything you have done so far, you act as though it will work, but you don't expect or need it to work. That is, you act as though you can manifest at will, with the aid of the Angel, but you don't care at all whether or not the magick works. The point of this Protocol is not to get the results, but to make the magickal effort. In doing so, you engage with the Angel so directly that you become at one with the Angel's reality.

Think of something that you want to change. It can be something that matters to you a great deal, or something of limited importance, but it should be something that has meaning for you. Don't try to manifest a pair of striped socks because you think it would be an interesting way to test the magick. Think of something that you actually want to change. It doesn't have to be the most meaningful and important thing in your life. If you want the traffic to be lighter than usual this morning, that's a genuine need, something you want.

You can work with all forms of change, either trying to affect the outer world, or your relationship to it. You may want to attract something specific, or you may want to change an aspect of yourself.

Remember that manifesting at will means causing change through an act of decision. It doesn't mean you are using force, or extreme willpower. It is the opposite of that. You show the Angel what you have chosen, you ask for it to become your reality, and then you move on with your life.

Although I call this a Protocol, it is even less ritualistic than other parts of the book because it can be done at any time, without anything other than a thought. You notice a desire, you notice what you want to change, and you offer your thoughts and feelings to the Angel. In that moment, you are communicating with the Angel. You are heard.

The challenge is to do this with conviction while simultaneously expecting nothing. You should be completely willing for your request for change to fail. Remember that you are doing this as part of your work to reach the Guardian Angel, and as such, if there is something you really want to change, you might prefer to use other magick. If so, you can always ask the Angel to bless your magick. That is one of the most effective ways I know to get a result of any kind. But for now, please keep in mind that manifesting at will, while not an experiment, is once more something like play. You are doing this as though it is certain to work, but then being completely relaxed about it not working. If it does work, of course, then celebrate that the Angel has helped, with a silent feeling of joy or approval.

This description is the shortest in the book because your experience will be so vital. Much more instruction would only confuse matters because they will be specific to your circumstances, place in life, desires, abilities, and the depth of your needs. All I will say is that you should not worry, and you can know that every time you do this (whether it is ten times a day or once a week), you bring the Angel into your life.

The Quest for Contact

When you have worked with the Seven Protocols for some time, I expect you will have an awareness of the Angel and a deeper connection to creating your own destiny at will. Some people will even achieve Complete Contact with the Angel, or something approaching that state, using nothing other than the Protocols.

You can choose to keep working with the Protocols, or you can let them go, knowing that the Angel will remain with you. Many people come to a point where they return to Protocol One, knowing that is a sufficient process to maintain the required level of contact. Others prefer to keep going with some or all of the Protocols to varying degrees. But what happens when you are seeking Complete Contact, where the Angel is as real and present as could ever be possible for you?

If you have come to this part of the book early, eager to achieve Complete Contact *before* you work with the Protocols, you can probably imagine that I will say impatience is a barrier to magick. You cannot force this magick to work faster. There are no rules, of course, and you are free to work with these methods should you feel ready for them, but please know that working with the Seven Protocols is the way to your Angel. What lies ahead involves an expansion and refinement of your inner energy.

Many people seek Complete Contact as a form of proof, reassurance, or confirmation of religious beliefs or supernatural expectations. I cannot say these are bad reasons, but I do know that when people are looking for proof, they are less likely to find it than people who seek contact with a sense of exploration and curiosity. The attainment of Complete Contact can result in beautiful and mystical experiences, but that is an effect rather than an aim. Your aim might be to seek the Angel's wisdom, to communicate directly regarding your problems, your plans, your expectations for growth, and your magickal needs.

Please recall what I said in earlier chapters about the nature of this contact being dictated largely by your imaginative style, as the imagination acts as both lens and filter for the experience. By now, you should have experienced benefits and insights from the Angel, and you can expect these to increase and improve if you choose to commit to a more direct connection with the Angel.

I will reiterate that although Complete Contact can now be your aim, you are not seeking a spectacular moment of revelation. In truth, many people *will* experience such a moment, but it should not be sought. Complete Contact occurs in varying degrees and can be obtained in ways that feel vague or hazy at first. Imagine the difference between watching a beautiful film on a huge cinema screen and watching a home video on a small phone. Although the experience may be smaller at first, that does not make it less real.

There is a certain degree of irony in calling this stage of the magick a quest. As you are fully aware, I believe that contact is already underway as soon as you think about it. I also believe that achieving Complete Contact does not need to be an ordeal. It will not occur because you perform a mighty climactic ritual. It is, however, a quest in the sense that you don't say a few magick words and get a result a couple of days later. You know you are undertaking something more substantial, and so calling it a quest is accurate. But try to see the quest as an adventure rather than a trial.

The Quest for Contact may be more intense than what has gone before, but it is not overly complicated or demanding, and you can expect to see improvements in your ability to experience feelings of bliss as you progress.

I mentioned that you might stop using the Protocols if that feels right, but my personal advice is to continue with Protocol One, each day at the least, as you work through The Quest for

Contact. Despite its simplicity, it remains one of the most useful aspects of this process. Perform Protocol One before you work with one of the sigils, and you have made a strong overture to the Angel that can help energise the magick between you.

The sigils included in the following pages are the most powerful I know for aiding this work directly. They have other uses, but used in this context, they improve your ability to become aware of your Angel, and that will assist your desire to bring about Complete Contact.

I said at the beginning of the book that you can't just use a few magick words and stare at some pretty sigils to obtain your Angel, and that remains true. These sigils are not magick keys that give you access to your Angel. They assist you in entering a state where you are open to the Angel. That means they bring about changes within you that improve your ability to achieve contact. You are not unlocking a secret gateway to the Angel but opening energy gateways within yourself and reducing any sense of separation through a shift in perspective.

There are two levels of energy explored here, and each has subtle layers of power within that help to open up your reality. Once again, I suggest working through these in order, although there is no set timeline. I do, however, warn against using all seven sigils in the next seven days, or even worse, on a single day. It's not that you'll be overwhelmed with magickal energy, but that in attempting too much, you'll probably be underwhelmed by nothing happening.

My experience and observation have shown that the response you obtain from these sigils will be anything but predictable. Sometimes you feel nothing, and often the energy is subtle. At other times, it can be so powerful you feel speechless. You know by now to expect nothing but allow anything, and remember you are safe because the Angel is supporting your journey.

Some people want to use energy-raising from the outset and will come to this part of the book immediately. They will start using these sigils from day one. I believe this is because The Bornless Ritual, described earlier, was a popular way for people to feel like something was happening. Even though it's just a modified exorcism, it does create strange feelings, and that makes people feel like magickal progress is being made, whether it is or not. And so, energy-raising rituals are popular, and I know some people will want them as soon as possible. I cannot stop that, and there may be no need to. But if you are too eager, note all that I have said about impatience. And as always, remember that I also encourage experimentation. Once again, this contradiction is not as bizarre as it may sound.

Remember, however, that no matter how powerful these sigils may feel, they are refining your energy. This process integrates your energy with Angelic energy, raising you to a level where sensing and knowing the Angel becomes complete.

The first two sigils work on the first energy level and are quite simple. They will be familiar to many magickal workers. The first contains the Seventy-Two Letter Name of God arranged around a blank circle. The second contains the Seventy-Two Names of God arranged around a blank circle. Both of these sigils are written in Hebrew and are based on names, words, and well-established occult knowledge. You do not need to know Hebrew, as the letters are used as a visual encoding of magickal effect, and gazing at the sigils as instructed will bring out their power.

For the second energy level, there are five sigils that contain patterns of Enochian letters. I have described Enochian as being like a source code of magick, reaching into the fundamental structures of reality. As such, a well-designed Enochian sigil can make a tremendous change in your relationship with magick power. Despite the simplicity of what is presented, I am sure you will sense the energy contained within them.

I covered the history and meaning of Enochian in my book, *Success Magick*. That exploration was quite brief because the book is directed at practical magic, but if you want to know more about the origins of Enochian, it will give you some insight into how these sigils were constructed. For the sake of this book, you only need to know that each sigil opens an energy gateway via six Aethyrs, which are heavens with various qualities and powers. The first sigil, for example, contains the Aethyrs known as LIL, ARN, ZOM, PAZ, LIT, and MAZ. Enochian is a strange and glorious language, but on the page, when written in English, it can look quite puerile. Heavens with names such as POP or ZIM do not sound impressive or magickal. Although I list the names of the Aethyrs for each sigil, I recommend working with the sigil itself, bringing your attention to it as will be described, rather than trying to read the letters. Despite this, you might be frustrated if I never even showed you how the letters are organised, so this is an overview of the angelical alphabet:

You don't need to understand this at all, but it's provided so that you're not left completely in the dark. If you study the sigils, you will see that the names of the Aethyrs are written in the outer ring, while the coded patterns of letters appear in the central section. For this to work, you don't need to know anything except that it's safe and also contains a power that is usually described as being obviously magickal. Most people find that working with Enochian sigils is one of the fastest ways to sense and expand magickal energy.

The first sigil you work with starts with the heaven known as LIL, and the final sigil ends with the heaven known as TEX. If you know anything about Enochian, you will know that people often work with the Aethyrs in the other direction, going from TEX to LIL, aiming to go from the earthly to the heavenly. In much of our magick, we reverse this, starting at an elevated place (which is completely attainable) and then bringing the magick down to the level of ordinary existence. This is particularly useful with Guardian Angel magick, where you are aiming to fuse your experience of the Angel (which is essentially supernatural) with your ordinary life.

All these sigils work even if you know nothing about their origins, and that is what I hope you will soon discover. Although the first two are bold in their simplicity, that is exactly the point. A blank space in the centre of those circles represents the space where you interact with your Angel, and you are encircled by a magickal interaction with Divinity. The Enochian sigils are also relatively simple in visual terms, but they will bring a potent amplification to your perception of inner energy.

You will be shown how to use these sigils in the coming pages but remember that this is not a way to force the Angel out of some hazy netherworld. The Angel is with you, and by clarifying your energy in this way, you bring Complete Contact closer with every moment.

Energy Raising – Level One

Keep in mind that you are not raising magickal energy for the sake of it, but for the sake of contact and to clarify your connection with your Angel.

In Level One, there are two sigils. You may prefer to work with the first for some time before working with the second. Many people then find that using both on the same day is beneficial, but trust your own feelings on this matter.

There is more of a sense of ritual with the remaining parts of the book, and you will get the best results if you can find a time and place to be undisturbed. The work may only take a few minutes, so this should not be too hard to find. You may find it becomes easier to work for longer as you get used to the energy, but there is no need to aim for long sessions. You may feel the energies, or you may feel nothing at all. What matters is that in going through this process, your energy is being refined whether or not you feel it. You should notice your connection to the Angel increasing in the days and weeks that follow as you continue to use this method.

To begin, become clear in your intention to make contact with the Angel, and then let go of the need for a response, sign, or any given result. Know that you are going to work with magickal energies, accessed through the sigil, but again let go of the need to have any particular experience.

You now gaze softly at the white space in the centre of the sigil. You are not trying to read the letters, study their shapes, or observe anything; instead, your gaze rests on the white space. If your eyes flit around and look at other parts of the sigil, that is fine, and you only need to bring them back to the white space, gently and without any concern.

You are only letting your eyes gaze at the white space and as you do this, the sigil is drawn within you, and its work begins. The letters that are in your peripheral vision are taken within you, and they begin to do their work.

Do not try to generate or imagine the energy, but remain aware of your mind, your body, your breathing, and notice if anything changes. You may feel anything from a change in temperature to a strong emotional shift, or a difference in the quality of light. Energy shifts manifest in a thousand different ways. Keep your Angel in mind because when your energy is raised, moments of contact can occur.

Continue for as long as feels comfortable, and when you decide to stop, do so with a feeling of completion. That is, do not stop and wonder whether it's worked, or whether it was a waste of time. Instead, allow yourself to feel that it was worthwhile and that progress toward your Angel has been achieved.

These instructions apply to the next two sigils. You can perform these energy-raising rituals immediately before or after the Protocols, or at any other time.

The First Sigil of Contact

This sigil contains The Seventy-Two Letter Name of God, derived from various kabbalistic sources. The Name is written in Hebrew, running counter-clockwise. The first letters in the ring are upright, becoming inverted at the base of the sigil. You can study and examine the sigil as much as you like but during the ritual, let your gaze rest on the white space so that the letters are at the periphery of your vision.

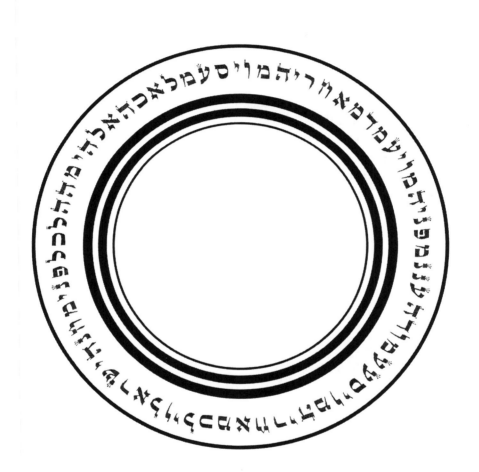

119

The Second Sigil of Contact

This sigil contains The Seventy-Two Names of God. Each of these Hebrew Names is comprised of three letters, and each begins with a letter originating from The Seventy-Two Letter Name of God. The letters of each Name are arranged one on top of the other, oriented towards the centre of the sigil. The order of the names moves counter-clockwise, with the Names being upright at first and inverted at the base. The central space is white, and this is where your gaze will rest during the ritual.

The letters in this sigil, especially those from the inner circle, may appear quite small. Do not be concerned that they are too small. If you look at the size of the letters you are reading now, they are probably smaller than the letters in the sigil. If you are using a tiny phone screen, you may want to zoom in and look at the image first so that you have seen all the letters clearly, but if you are using the paperback, hardback, or an ordinary device, there is no need to get closer or try to examine the detail.

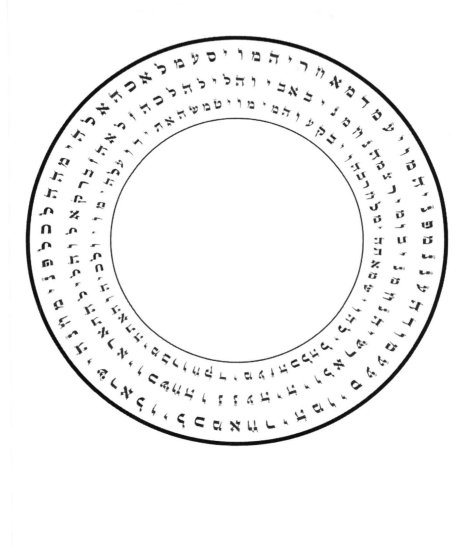

Energy Raising – Level Two

There are five Enochian sigils in this part of the book. I consider these to be the most powerful way to refine your inner energy, but please note that this is no substitute for the other magickal work. If you have progressed with the Protocols, these sigils can bring clarity to your connection with the Angel. Your initial experience may not be as tangible as you expect, and regular work is recommended to become familiar with the energies. Much depends on who you are, where you are in your journey, and how you have travelled through this magick. Be willing to continue with all the work you find in this book, rather than trying to get it over with.

Each of the five sigils has a slightly different energy quality, and generally, the intensity of the energy increases as you progress. Whatever you experience is fine. I have added brief notes about the content of each sigil. This is only for those who are interested. If you have no interest in that, just use the sigil, because the book is about using the magick.

The first Enochian sigil in this book is called The Third Sigil of Contact. When you feel you have gained something from it, you can move on to the next, and so on. You are free to combine several rituals each day, but I strongly recommend working through these in order, taking it as slowly as you are willing to go, in order to sense the subtle changes that occur, as well as the less subtle ones.

To begin the ritual, become clear in your intention to make contact with the Angel, and then let go of the need for a response, sign, or any given result. Know that you are going to work with magickal energies, accessed through the sigil, but let go of the need to have any particular experience.

Scan your eyes around the perimeter of the outer circle, moving them anti-clockwise three or four times. Do this slowly. You are not reading, or trying to study detail, so let your focus be on the white space between the letters. Your gaze can be soft and relaxed, with your eye movement smooth.

When that is done, let your gaze rest on the very centre of the sigil, where all the lines converge. Keep your eyes on that point, gently and without staring. You will find that your eyes drift around and that some of the shapes and letters come into focus. You may even sense light lifting from the sigil. Do not be alarmed, and do not be concerned if none of this happens.

As before, the sigil is drawn within you, and its work begins. Remain aware of your mind, your body, your breathing, and notice if anything changes, if any energy arises, but keep your eyes on the sigil. They don't have to be locked on, and there should be no force, but let the sigil remain in view, with your focus on the converging lines.

The energies of these sigils can be quite noticeable. If you feel the energy, do not fight it, but let yourself notice it moving through you.

Continue for as long as feels comfortable, and when you decide to stop, do so with a feeling of completion. Allow yourself to know that it was worthwhile and that progress toward your Angel has been achieved.

These instructions apply to all the sigils that follow. You can perform these energy-raising rituals immediately before or after the Protocols, or at any other time.

The Third Sigil of Contact

This Sigil presents an Enochian Gateway comprised of six Aethyrs, being LIL, ARN, ZOM, PAZ, LIT, and MAZ. The letters run counter-clockwise, being upright at the start, inverting as they reach the base.

The nine letters arranged around the lines of the central pattern are Don, Gisg, Drux, Gon, Na, Gal, Tal, Or, and Med. The letters are all upright, and their arrangement echoes codes expressed within the Enochian Tables of Loagaeth.

When you have scanned your eyes over the sigil as instructed, your gaze will rest on the centre of the circle where the lines converge.

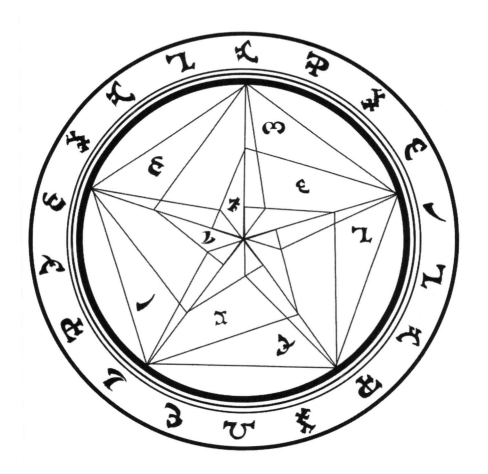

127

The Fourth Sigil of Contact

This Sigil presents an Enochian Gateway comprised of six Aethyrs, being DEO, ZID, ZIP, ZAX, ICH, and LOE. The letters run counter-clockwise, being upright at the start, inverting as they reach the base.

The nine letters arranged around the lines of the central pattern are Van, Don, Fam, Drux, Veh, Med, Gal, Ceph, and Un. The letters are all upright, and their arrangement echoes codes expressed within the Enochian Tables of Loagaeth.

When you have scanned your eyes over the sigil as instructed, your gaze will rest on the centre of the circle where the lines converge.

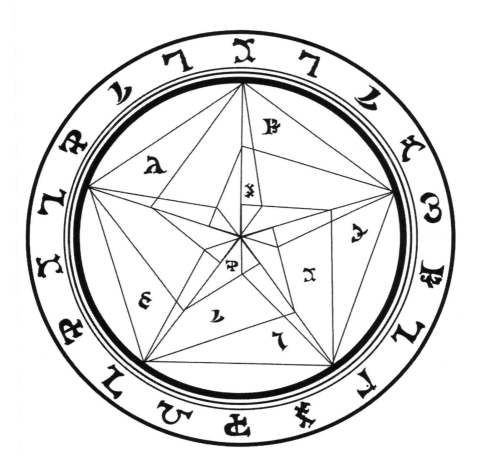

129

The Fifth Sigil of Contact

This Sigil presents an Enochian Gateway comprised of six Aethyrs, being ZIM, UTA, OXO, LEA, TAN, and ZEN. The letters run counter-clockwise, being upright at the start, inverting as they reach the base.

The nine letters arranged around the lines of the central pattern are Gon, Don, Ur, Tal, Mals, Pa, Med, Drux, and Graph. The letters are all upright, and their arrangement echoes codes expressed within the Enochian Tables of Loagaeth.

When you have scanned your eyes over the sigil as instructed, your gaze will rest on the centre of the circle where the lines converge.

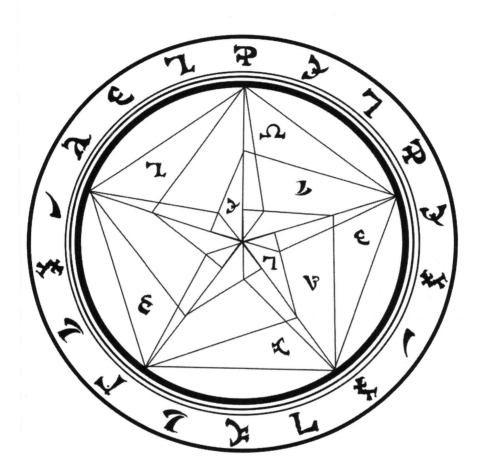

The Sixth Sigil of Contact

This Sigil presents an Enochian Gateway comprised of six Aethyrs, being POP, CHR, ASP, LIN, TOR, and NIA. The letters run counter-clockwise, being upright at the start, inverting as they reach the base.

The nine letters arranged around the lines of the central pattern are Ur, Tal, Gal, Van, Fam, Un, Gon, Med, and Graph. The letters are all upright, and their arrangement echoes codes expressed within the Enochian Tables of Loagaeth.

When you have scanned your eyes over the sigil as instructed, your gaze will rest on the centre of the circle where the lines converge.

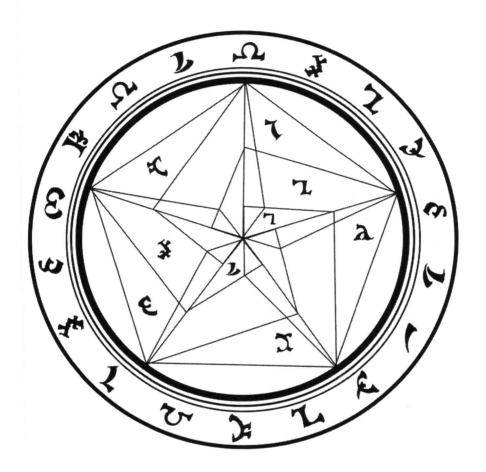

The Seventh Sigil of Contact

This Sigil presents an Enochian Gateway comprised of six Aethyrs, being UTI, DES, ZAA, BAG, RII, and TEX. The letters run counter-clockwise, being upright at the start, inverting as they reach the base.

The nine letters arranged around the lines of the central pattern are Gon, Na, Or, Un, Gon, Don, Ceph, Un, and Ur. The letters are all upright, and their arrangement echoes codes expressed within the Enochian Tables of Loagaeth.

When you have scanned your eyes over the sigil as instructed, your gaze will rest on the centre of the circle where the lines converge.

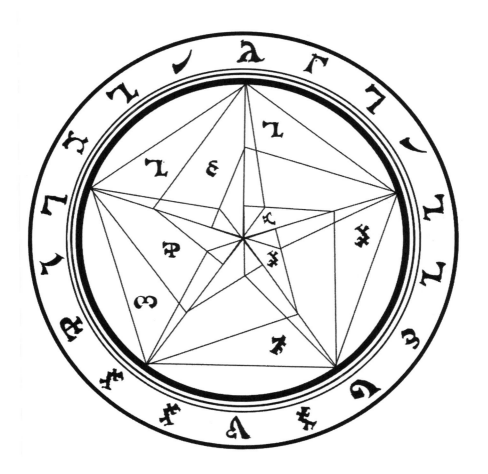

135

Additional Thoughts

At some point, you may give up this work. That may be because you have lost interest, lost hope, or become skeptical. It may seem that nothing much is happening. The magick may feel less powerful than you hoped. You may feel a sense of anger and wasted time. This is an ordinary part of the process, and if you stop for a while, that is fine.

I trust that should you give up, you will return to the magick, strengthened, and with more insight into how it can and will work for you.

You may also give up because you find the instructions baffling. I have always tried to be clear when I write, but as I said at the beginning, it is impossible to be too clear-cut or instructive with this subject. And while I have said that the old methods are too complicated, with too much detail, too much demand on your time, and too much disruption, you may feel that I have gone too far the other way. I have left you with too much to work out for yourself. Please trust me when I say this is the only way it can be.

I believe that you will find your way to the Angel, and that if you have begun to work with the magick in this book, you will sense this to be true.

For the readers who have been asking for this book for many years, I am grateful for your patience and excited to know what you will become.

If you have already achieved Complete Contact with your Angel, the journey is far from over. As you begin to communicate, you will see how much further you can go, and you will also know that I cannot lead you there. The connection will continue to evolve if you continue to nourish it. Maintain contact with your Angel, and the connection will always reward you.

If you have not progressed that far, it may be through choice, or it may be because things are not progressing as fast as you want. Be content, but also be open to change and know that what you are uncovering here is one of the most profound mystical experiences you could ever have while also being the strongest way to express practical magick. I wish you all the best in this journey and admire you for taking the first steps.

Damon Brand

Further Reading

The magick revealed in this book works effectively for most people, but if in doubt, The Gallery of Magick website is an excellent source of background material and practical posts that help you to get magick working. We could have published two or three books on magickal practice, but instead, it's all there for free.

You can also find extensive **FAQs** for every book. I urge you to make good use of the site when you encounter problems, and also when you wish to expand your understanding of magick.

I hope you use and enjoy the sigils in this book. They are not in the public domain, so they should not be used for resale of any kind. To make personal copies, you can photocopy, photograph, or take screenshots and print them out, but I recommend using them on a device, computer screen, or in the paperback or hardback.

Please note that we only have one official Facebook page, and information in various fan groups is not always accurate. Also, please note that the Gallery of Magick authors are Damon Brand, Adam Blackthorne, Gordon Winterfield, and Zanna Blaise.

If you have an interest in developing your magick further, there are many texts from The Gallery of Magick authors that can assist you.

Magickal Protection is used to make your life and magick safe and also frees you from negativity. It gives all your magick more power. The book contains rituals that can be directed at specific problems, as well as a daily practice called The Sword Banishing, which is one of our most popular and effective rituals.

The 72 Angels of Magick helps you discover the secrets of angelic power. The angels are ready to listen and ready to work for you. All you have to do is ask in the right way. You don't need to believe anything or belong to any religion. You don't need to be pure or worthy. All you need is a strong desire for something to change in your world. If you have that desire, the angels will take you where you want to go. It is their purpose to give you the power to express the life you dream of living.

The Angels of Alchemy works on personal transformation, revealing the powers of forty-two angels to restore confidence, inspire your thoughts, find patience, provide emotional balance, and give insight into your life. This can be the key to unlocking magick.

Archangels of Magick is Damon Brand's masterwork of practical magick. It has been described as, 'A masterpiece with no equal. The ONE book that you absolutely MUST add to your library.' The book contains simple methods for calling on the archangels, along with methods for invocation, and the direct contact of evocation. There's enough detail to thrill experts, and it's completely suitable for beginners.

Magickal Cashbook uses a ritual to attract small bursts of money out of the blue and works best not when you are desperate, but when you can approach the magick with a sense of enjoyment and pleasure.

Magickal Riches is more comprehensive, with rituals for everything from gambling to sales. There is a master ritual to oversee magickal income, and it contains the most treasured secrets of practical money magick. It should be considered essential reading for anybody with an interest in financial magick.

Wealth Magick is for the more ambitious and contains a complex set of rituals for earning money by building a career. This is a long-term working for serious occultists who turn the focus of their life to wealth creation.

The Magickal Job Seeker helps when you're looking for work or a change of job. In the reviews, people say that after months of searching, jobs come in days.

The Master Works of Chaos Magick is an overview of self-directed and creative magick. It provides an alternative approach to magick, with experimental ideas and a new way to work with the legendary Olympic Spirits.

The 72 Sigils of Power provides you with over three hundred powers to work on inner magick for outer change. It reveals the power of Contemplation Magic (for insight and wisdom) and Results Magic (for changing the world around you).

Words of Power is the best book for fast and easy magickal results. If you're new to magick, there's no better place to start. There are rituals for protection, gaining an advantage, appearing valuable, finding success, and many more.

The Greater Words of Power contains thirty-one Archangel rituals that help with creativity, influence, personal transformation, emotions, and the mind. The magick is simple, direct, and effective.

Magickal Servitors directs you to create spirits that work your magick for you, so you can obtain precise, targeted results. There are countless books and free websites that will tell you how to create a servitor. This book contains two major secrets discovered by The Gallery of Magick. These secrets are embedded within the fabric of this process. The magick is designed to be easy for beginners as well as experienced occultists.

Demons of Magick is Gordon Winterfield's modern masterpiece of dark magick, covering three new ways to evoke and command the seventy-two demons of Goetia. The magick of demons can lead to a life of success, power, and extraordinary peace. Demons will demolish enemies, enrich bold ventures, satisfy material desires, and provide you with wisdom, charisma, healing, and persuasive dignity. If these are works of darkness, they bring great light.

Angels of Wrath is not a book of casual curses, but a book of peace and justice. Angels are powerful beings that can be called to work great and wrathful wonders. Whether you are new to magick or quite experienced, this book will introduce you to a lesser-known group of angels. When called in combination, these angels have the power to cause devastation to your enemies.

Mystical Words of Power reveals a ground-breaking form of magick. It's easy to use but works in a completely new way. In Part One, there are seven major rituals covering Perception, Knowledge, Imagination, Love, Healing, Transformation, and The Empowered Mind. In Part Two, you can direct the magick where you want. There are over fifty sigils to fine-tune your reality. One reviewer said, 'This book is something else. The workings in part one of the book have been my most powerful results to date.'

Sigils of Power and Transformation has brought great results to many people, proving to be our most popular and well-loved book. There are 111 sigils for health, luck, money, and much more. There are no angels, demons, or any spirits in this direct magick. One reviewer said, 'This book of Sigils works. Sometimes instantly. More often with a deep, subtle power that gradually shapes your reality in a few days according to your exact wishes yet beyond your expectations.'

Success Magick is Damon Brand's revolutionary work of Enochian Magick. The great secrets of magick were delivered to a genius mathematician in the Sixteenth Century. After that, the magick was locked away for many years, then found again and shared in secret. Occultists have unraveled these secrets to the point where they have become practical. The methods described here are based on a lifetime of studying and exploring success, combined with the wisdom of the Enochian Angels.

www.galleryofmagick.com

Damon Brand

Made in the USA
Las Vegas, NV
20 February 2022